JESTING MOSES

JESTING MOSES

A Study in Cabellian Comedy

by ARVIN R. WELLS

UNIVERSITY OF FLORIDA PRESS

Gainesville, 1962

A University of Florida Press Book

COPYRIGHT, 1962, BY THE BOARD OF COMMISSIONERS

OF STATE INSTITUTIONS

OF FLORIDA

LIBRARY OF CONGRESS

CATALOGUE CARD No. 62-20737

PRINTED BY ROBINSONS INC.

ORLANDO, FLORIDA

To
Jeanne Livingston Wells

Preface

For nearly thirty years now James Branch Cabell
has remained on the ultimate periphery of critical attention. In
1959 the last of his novels to remain in print, *Jurgen,* was dropped
from the Penguin list; his works are no longer before the public.
He has not, however, at any time been wholly forgotten. He has
survived as an object of admiration for a small, scattered group of
devoted Cabellians and as an object of attack for the majority of
critics who, since 1930, have undertaken to assess the literature of
the 1920's.

It is the implicit contention of this study that survival upon such
precarious terms is less than Cabell deserves. It seems fair to say
that rarely has a serious literary artist had so little luck in finding a
responsive, judicious, and articulate audience. The study which
follows is an attempt—almost the first extended attempt—to cut
through the prejudices, both pro and con, that have obscured Cabell's
accomplishment and to examine intently the actual substance of that
accomplishment. If it succeeds in demonstrating that Cabell's works
do in fact reward such attention, it will, in the author's eyes, have
justified its existence.

It remains to give special thanks to Professor Joe Lee Davis of the University of Michigan for having first directed my attention to James Branch Cabell, to Mrs. Margaret Freeman Cabell for granting me permission to quote at large from the published works of James Branch Cabell, and to the Ohio University Research Committee for providing the assistance that has made this publication possible.

I wish also to make acknowledgment for permission to quote from the following works still in copyright: to Barnes and Noble, Inc., for permission to quote from *The Philosophy of "As If"* by Hans Vaihinger, trans. C. K. Ogden; to Doubleday and Company, Inc., for permission to quote from *The American Novel and Its Tradition* by Richard Chase, copyright, 1957, by Richard Chase; to James A. Feibleman and Russell and Russell, Inc., for permission to quote from *In Praise of Comedy* by James A. Feibleman; to the Estate of Lane Cooper for permission to quote from *An Aristotelian Theory of Comedy* by Lane Cooper; to Harvard University Press for permission to quote from *The Dark Voyage and the Golden Mean* by Albert Cook; to Henry Regnery Company for permission to quote from *The Modern Novel in America* by Frederick J. Hoffman; to Alfred A. Knopf, Inc., for permission to quote from *Essays and Soliloquies* by Miguel de Unamuno, trans. J. E. Crawford Fitch; to The Library of Living Philosophers for permission to quote from *The Philosophy of George Santayana*, ed. Paul Arthur Schlipp; to Macmillan Company for permission to quote from *The Great Tradition* by Granville Hicks and *Intellectual America* by Oscar Cargill; to Charles Scribner's Sons for permission to quote from *Soliloquies in England and later Soliloquies, The Life of Reason: Reason in Society,* and *The Winds of Doctrine* by George Santayana; to the Yale University Press for permission to quote from *Unamuno* by Arturo Barea; and to the University of New Mexico Press for permission to quote from *Carl Van Vechten and the Twenties* by Edward Lueders.

ARVIN R. WELLS

Ohio University
Athens, Ohio

Contents

It cannot well have escaped your notice, Messire, since you also were once a poet, that it is the function of every verbal artist thus to admit others into a world, and into a manner of living, which he admires, without admitting himself. He remains a lesser Moses upon a more tiny Pisgah, appreciately to observe, and in due course to record, the conduct of those ephemeral tribes whom his labors have introduced into the Promised Land.

LADIES AND GENTLEMEN

The Cabell Problem

Between 1905 and 1955 James Branch Cabell published more than forty books, not counting the extensively revised second and third editions of many of these. He published his first story in 1901 and his final volume, a brief memoir, in 1955. During the first thirty years of his writing career, he conceived and executed an elaborate literary plan which took final shape in the eighteen-volume Storisende edition of *The Biography of Manuel.*

The Biography of Manuel is Cabell's major achievement. Into it flowed all of the creative and intellectual energies of thirty years of professional writing, and in the composition of it Cabell elaborated a point of view which is unique at least in American literature, and developed a distinctive literary technique as a means of expressing this point of view. What he wrote later added nothing new to his store of ideas and techniques. Taken separately, the books after 1930 are often entertaining and clever, but ranged alongside of the Biography they take on the appearance of somewhat flat and unnecessary addenda. Consequently, these later books are significant to the student of Cabell primarily for the light which they incidentally throw upon the themes and techniques of the major work.

1

The lengthy and elaborately planned *Biography of Manuel,* on the other hand, demands close critical and scholarly attention. Not, of course, that mere bulk and elaborateness by themselves have any special claim upon the scholar and critic, but when a large body of works has been produced by an artist of integrity, then the claim may be said to be established. James Branch Cabell gave evidence of his integrity in one of the few ways open to the artist: he went his own way, elaborating his own concepts and techniques, without reference to the noisy ebb and flow of the tides of taste. Moreover, he brought into American literature a set of attitudes and a point of view that cannot be dismissed out of hand. Yet, as a matter of fact, Cabell has to date received very little thorough critical or scholarly attention.

During the 1920's Cabell was, to be sure, the subject of numerous critical reviews and comments, but these were seldom analytical. They were likely to be either broadly laudatory or broadly damning. On the whole the writers of these articles and reviews assumed beforehand that Cabell had either great merit or no merit at all, and they proceeded to elaborate their enthusiasms or antipathies more or less impressionistically. Even the few more extended studies—for example, Warren McNeill's *Cabellian Harmonics,* H. L. Mencken's *James Branch Cabell,* and Carl Van Doren's *James Branch Cabell*— while they point to possible critical approaches, do in fact merely glance over the surface of Cabell's works. Of all those who wrote about Cabell, only Parrington in his essay, "The Incomparable Mr. Cabell," attempted to take full account of the complexities and significance of Cabell's thought and method. This is not to say that Parrington thoroughly carried out what he attempted; he, like the other admirers of Cabell, was betrayed into hyperbolic praise by his enthusiasm—an enthusiasm which hurt his reputation without ultimately helping Cabell's.

Actually the whole Cabell controversy of the twenties, especially the enthusiastic support which he then received, has merely served to obscure the fact of neglect. It has created the impression that Cabell was a faddish, popular novelist who, like all such novelists, has merely fallen victim to the vagaries of popular taste, and it has allowed the later critics, most of whom have been eager to dismiss Cabell, to assume that he has had his trial, has been tried and found wanting.

As a result those who have wanted to dismiss Cabell, but have not been able to ignore him, have not felt obliged to examine him closely. Granville Hicks in *The Great Tradition* is satisfied with an almost *ad hominem* attack: "He is a sleek, smug egoist, whose desire to be a gentleman of the old school breeds dissatisfaction with the existing order, but who has not enough imaginative vigor to create a robust world in which deeds of chivalry and gallantry are performed. Instead, he has written mild little fantasies, carefully baited with obscenities. His whole work is a structure of lies, from his tinselled style to his theorizing on life and literature."[1] Such a comment as this may summarize Cabell's personality, though this is doubtful, but it certainly will not serve as a critical appraisal of his works. It does, of course, reveal the underlying source of Hicks' animosity.

In 1941 Oscar Cargill in *Intellectual America*[2] took up the attack and attempted to annihilate Cabell's claim to attention by exposing the sources of Cabell's attitudes and theories, by tracing his literary lineage back to discredited ancestors—Edgar Saltus, Robert Louis Stevenson, and the writers of "Graustark romance." As far as this analysis goes it is accurate, but, of course, it is not an inclusive survey of the influences which have at one time or another helped to shape Cabell's development. Moreover, to base a critical evaluation, as Cargill does, at least by implication, upon the sources of a work rather than upon the work itself is an obviously fallacious procedure. It is as if one were to argue that the Ganges is a mountain stream because it has its source in the Himalayas.

As deficient and unsatisfactory as are the appraisals of Hicks and Cargill, they are fairly representative of the tenor of such critical attention as Cabell did receive during the thirties and forties. Sometimes the note of belligerent antipathy is replaced by a note of regret, but the conclusion is essentially the same: ". . . he is a trifler and will not come in from play."[3] . . . "If he survives the waning notoriety of *Jurgen*, it will be as a museum piece representing the psychology of a Virginian who would be an intellectual leader yet had not quite what it takes."[4] . . . "Its [*Jurgen's*] popularity, like the success of other Cabell novels, can only be ascribed to the fact that its public was caught gratefully off guard, that they thought they had found a deeper meaning than was actually there, and that the principal attractiveness of the fantasy was erotic."[5] To date relatively little has been said about what actually is there.

Recently, however, there has been some stirring of renewed interest in Cabell. Edward Wagenknecht in *The Calvacade of the American Novel,*[6] Edd Winfield Parks in *Southern Renascence,*[7] and Edmund Wilson in a lengthy article in the popular *New Yorker* magazine[8] have all called for a re-evaluation, a reopening of the case. In the meanwhile Cabell has been quietly consigned to the museum of curios left behind by the "fantastic twenties." Of course, he had spent a long apprenticeship and had published some of his major works before the twenties began; yet it was in the twenties that he found such audience as he enjoyed, and his identification with this period has been something of a service, though it is hardly full justice. It at least rescues him from the category of freakish anomaly and suggests a firmer basis for his popularity than an audience "caught gratefully off guard." But on the debit side it leads to a restricted categorical view of Cabell as a member of a group or participant in a movement: he belongs with the "exquisites," the escapists, the decadents, the iconoclasts, and all such breeds as perished in the great avalanche of 1929. Of course, Cabell himself subscribed to some such view when in *These Restless Heads* he predicted the decline and fall of his own literary generation. He based his prediction upon the observation that the writers of the twenties had offered no constructive program, no panacea; their job had been that of the iconoclast—the clearing away of taboos and the smashing of no longer efficacious idols. Their tone had been predominantly ironic or sarcastic. For such a generation as Cabell describes, he spoke in key; he belonged; but the fact of his belonging does not necessarily warrant the conclusion arrived at by John Bellamy. Mr. Bellamy argues that a Cabell revival is extremely improbable, for, "While it is true that the gap between the popular and the cultivated taste is as wide as ever, iconoclasm and cynicism have gone out of fashion. Indeed, the intellectual of mid-century seeks as fanatically for faith as his counterpart in the twenties sought to avoid it."[9]   A revival, I take it, means not only a return to popularity but a beginning of serious critical attention.   If so, then Mr. Bellamy's judgment amounts to one more dismissal for Cabell.

Such a judgment reflects an oversimplification of Cabell if not of his audience.   It is true that in part Cabell spoke to and for the twenties, but the twenties were not merely iconoclastic.   They were marked not only by a desire to discredit and have done with those illusions (ideals and values) which seemed to have cheated and misled, but also by a struggle to discover an appropriate attitude to assume toward a world in which suddenly all oracles had ceased and all values become suspect.   Cabell's works were and are relevant to this struggle which had its origin in the nineteenth century and which continues.

Furthermore, if Cabell is related to the iconoclasts and so-called decadents of the 1920's, he is also related by his preoccupations and concepts to the highly diversified "tribe of reactionaries" who, in this country and abroad in the late nineteenth century, began a more or less sustained counterattack upon the all but triumphant forces of scientism and of its literary lieutenant, naturalism.   This tribe has included among others such men as Santayana, Bergson, Wallace Stevens, Anatole France—a sufficiently inharmonious, yet related group; and it is surprising to note at how many points Cabell betrays intellectual and imaginative affinities with this group.   Like others of these reactionaries, he has, as Parrington has pointed out, achieved a world-view which is a sort of lopsided compromise between idealism and naturalism.

Moreover, far from being anomalous, Cabell's works stand close to, if not within, one of the major traditions in American literature— the tradition of what Richard Chase has defined as the romance- novel.   "Let me say that the word [romance as used in romance- novel] must signify, besides the more obvious qualities of the picturesque and the heroic, an assumed freedom from the ordinary novelistic requirements of verisimilitude, development and conti- nuity; a tendency toward melodrama and idyl; a more or less formal abstractness and, on the other hand, a tendency to plunge into the underside of consciousness; a willingness to abandon moral questions or to ignore the spectacle of man in society, or to consider these things only indirectly and abstractly."[10] Cabell has extended this tradition, which already claims, according to Chase, the trans-Jamesian realm, to the realm of fantasy.

This brief discussion of critical attitudes toward and judgments of Cabell's works should suggest that for all practical purposes he has been neglected, that the controversy of which he has been the center has been fought with generalizations rather than with the tools of careful scholarship and criticism, that his present classification is too narrow, and that, in general, his works have been subjected to much heat but relatively little critical understanding. As Wagenknecht, Parks, and Wilson have maintained, there is ground for reopening the Cabell case, for seeking a re-evaluation; but understanding—close reading and explication—must precede evaluative judgment.

Thus far the most substantial contributions to an understanding of Cabell's works have come from those who have devoted themselves either to the running down of the sources of borrowings and allusions or to the discussion of his world-view. Neither of these activities, however, can produce anything but fragmentary knowledge of limited value unless the sources are seen in relation to the world-view and both are seen in relation to a third fact: that Cabell wrote comedies. Whatever the source of the materials with which Cabell has worked, the important thing is that for him they became the materials of comedy, and it is equally important to remember that he gave his world-view its fullest expression in a series of symbolic and allegorical comedies which form the main strand of *The Biography of Manuel.* "Comedy" is Cabell's own descriptive term. It appears in the subtitles of most of the key works in the Biography: for example, *Figures of Earth: A Comedy of Appearances; Jurgen: A Comedy of Justice; The Cream of the Jest: A Comedy of Evasion;* but just what Cabell means by the term is not immediately apparent, nor has the meaning been elucidated by the criticism that has appended itself to Cabell's works.

As far back as 1920 John J. Gunther felt it necessary to remark: "It is important to remember that Cabell laughs. In rejecting contemporary thoughts and practices, in his decision that life is a pretty

sorry muddle, he never displays the savage intolerance of Artzyba-
shev nor the undiluted pessimism of Hardy or Conrad. He plays
with conventions, shatters illusions, dispels ideals—and then wrings
wry humor from the residue."[11] Also in 1920 Parrington published
his essay, "The Incomparable Mr. Cabell," in which he hailed Cabell
as "the supreme comic spirit thus far granted us."[12] Both Gunther
and Parrington in their respective articles maintained that there is
such a thing as a distinctly Cabellian comedy, but neither of them
took the time or space to define and explore it. In 1931, when the
reaction was setting in in full strength, Harlan Hatcher attempted
to dismiss the whole question of Cabellian comedy: "Mr. Cabell
tells that life is a comedy and the actors all alike except in costume.
I am not inclined to deny the discovery. I had even suspected it
before I read it in Shakespeare and Ecclesiastes. But if it is truth
it should be set forth in a pattern equally comic. I have searched
for this rare quality in my attempts to admire Mr. Cabell. I do not
find it; instead I find 'The Profits of Paper Selling.' I have come
reluctantly to suspect that the comedy of Mr. Cabell is not cosmic
in tone or proportion."[13]

For the rest, the corpus of Cabell criticism is sprinkled with
comments about "Cabell's comic vigor," his "fine and lovely irony,"
his "farcical fantasy" that is "faithful to the essence of medieval
humor," his humor that is "fanciful, light, mocking, and always pecul-
iarly Cabellian"; but nowhere is there a thoroughgoing attempt to
answer the basic questions: what does Cabell understand by
"comedy"? How is his concept of comedy related to his world-view?
How is his concept of comedy reflected in the style and structure of
his works? And, as a part of the last question, to what extent do
his works, considered chronologically, reflect growth and change in
concept and practice?

The purpose of this study is to attempt to provide answers to
these questions. Cabell nowhere explicitly and systematically explained his concept of comedy, either its form or its function. His
fullest explicit statement is given in "The Letter Dedicatory" to
The Lineage of Lichfield, and, while highly suggestive, this is
neither systematic nor complete. There are, however, besides this
one, numerous comments scattered through Cabell's works which

do bear directly and indirectly upon this subject, and by examining this material in the light of other more fully articulated theories of comedy—for example, those of Meredith, Feibleman, and Cook— it is possible to interpret such hints and suggestions as it contains. In other words, other theories of comedy may be used as reflectors, which by comparison and contrast reveal the outline of Cabell's concept and at the same time clarify what is distinctly Cabellian in it. Any tendency to extravagance in interpretation can be checked by reference to the comedies themselves. This is admittedly a delicate operation, but not an impossible one. Once the general concept has in this way been abstractly elaborated, the problem becomes one of examining the specific comedies in *The Biography of Manuel* for the purpose of determining how the concept is put into practice.

However, before even the first of the major questions can be answered, it is necessary to consider in some detail Cabell's worldview. For Cabell, comedy is inherent in the ordinary patterns of man's life, though the perception of it requires that these patterns be seen projected against a cosmic background. Consequently, in order to understand fully Cabell's concept of comedy, it is necessary first of all to understand his basic assumptions about the nature of that cosmic background and about man's relationship to it.

2

The World-View

       The general impression that Cabell's point of view is anachronistic, that his was "an essentially mediaeval mind," is a result of the failure to go beneath the surface of his work. It must arise from more or less exclusive concentration upon Cabell's borrowings from medieval romance and legend, upon the subtle though consciously produced archaic flavor of his style, and upon his penchant for the allegorical mode. Cabell himself apparently thought of his work as symbolic rather than allegorical, and, though the point is somewhat sticky, a case might be made. For the characters and situations in Cabell's novels tend to be suggestive rather than representative, and at least the important characters are interesting as personalities, quite apart from the burden of meaning which their actions are made to bear. At any rate, if one penetrates to the core of Cabell's thought, one is led to conclusions not unlike those reached by C. F. McIntyre: "His notion of vanity as the power that has drawn men up from gorillaship recalls Mandeville, his concept of an author in whose mind the romance of the world exists is a rewording of Berkeley. But in the essentials, like it or not, he is a child of this present age."[1]

These points of contact with eighteenth century thought are no doubt real enough (the eighteenth century was a period which strongly attracted Cabell's imagination), but they should not be allowed to obscure the essentials. In Cabell's works these apparently eighteenth century concepts exist in a context of assumptions and attitudes which essentially modifies them. This context derives from the late nineteenth and the twentieth centuries. Cabell shares Mandeville's estimate of the role of vanity, but the significance is less exclusively political and social. What Cabell stresses is the power of vanity to lead man to transcend himself, at least momentarily, by an excursion into the ideal. As for Berkeley's concept, Cabell never approaches it except playfully. This, like so many other human concepts, is a rather beautiful idea with which to divert oneself, and Cabell and his characters sometimes amuse themselves by playing with it, but it is never proposed as more than a rather fantastic possibility. Moreover, even if taken on faith, it could not have in the context of Cabell's total world-view the same implications as it had for Berkeley. Underlying Berkeley's thought is the assumption that the mind of God is orderly, purposeful, and benevolent; therefore, the belief that everything exists within the mind of God was for him comforting. For Cabell, however, the dreaming or thinking god would have to be Koschei, the god of things as they are, and to posit an existence dependent entirely upon that irresponsible and rather pedestrian demiurge would yield very little comfort.

Actually, it is precisely in his professed inability to find any moral order—or, in fact, any order at all—in the universe that Cabell breaks with eighteenth century thought and reveals his essential affinities with twentieth century thought. The structure of the universe, Cabell contends, is from a human point of view irrational and therefore incomprehensible. Even if there is some pattern in it, even if the laws which man imagines he finds operating in it are working toward some end, neither the pattern nor the end is knowable. Insofar as man can be aware of the universe, he is aware merely of a gratuitous repetition of the most stupendous pyrotechnics. "All about us flows and gyrates unceasingly the material universe—an endless inconceivable jumble of rotatory blazing gas and frozen spheres and detonating comets, where through spins earth like a frail midge."[2]

In this cosmic perspective man's position in the universe appears purely fortuitous and parasitic. He is a scarcely perceptible vortex in the general flux of the life force which seems itself an intruder in the universe, "like a bird striving to nest in a limitless engine, insanely building among moving wheels and cogs and pistons and pulley-belts, whose moving toward their proper and intended purposes inevitably sweeps away each nest before completion."[3] Moreover, so far as man can discover there is no intelligent force in the universe to which he can appeal, no substantial grounds for his dreams and ideals, all of which are infected with illusion. Even in relation to the life force of which he is a momentary expression, his function seems to be merely that of transmission and perpetuation. This view is implicit in most of Cabell's works and is more or less fully stated in *Beyond Life*. It is important, however, to remember that Cabell has tried to maintain a consistently skeptical attitude toward all questions of metaphysics and cosmology. He talks in his own person about the role of the artist and about the life and psychology of man in this world, but significantly he rarely discusses metaphysical questions without first assuming a mask. The most explicit statements of the cosmic view are either attributed to the whimsical, disillusioned, and rhetorical John Charteris or projected through the minds of other characters.

Such a view is not unfamiliar even in its detail. It lurks behind, and occasionally becomes explicit in, the writings of Stephen Crane, Theodore Dreiser, and Robinson Jeffers. It is a vision conjured up out of the fundamental assumptions of philosophical naturalism and colored with the appropriate emotion. It is, in general, the vision of reality with which thinking man in the twentieth century has had to come to terms, and a vision which Cabell apparently shares with the naturalists against whom he fulminates at some length and with whom he has often been contrasted. The Dreiser-Cabell antithesis early became a cliché of literary criticism.

Cabell's quarrel with the naturalists does not, in fact, involve the truth or falsehood of their philosophical assumptions. In *Some of Us* he takes pains to give even Dreiser his due. Though the tone is no doubt patronizing, he does express respect for the integrity of Dreiser's vision.[4] However, from Cabell's point of view, philosophical naturalism is probably only one more elaborate fiction among many others. This, of course, does not prevent the naturalistic vision of reality from serving effectively as the background of his thought and feeling. It has behind it the accumulative weight of science and of history; it is pervasive in the intellectual atmosphere of the twentieth century and therefore has first claim upon the minds of those who in the twentieth century turn their attention to the nature of the universe. Cabell's antipathy to literary naturalism, however, is real enough, and it arises out of his concern for the consequences of such a viewpoint: the impoverishment of life through the arbitrary restriction of the play of the imagination. In *The Cream of the Jest* Felix Kennaston discovers that the only truly tragic subject is the wholesale destruction of human dreams,[5] and a logical corollary of this discovery, which, though Cabell never states it, is implicit in all of his writings, is the belief that for man the worst possible fate would be the loss of his ability to believe in the constructions of his own imagination. Such a loss disturbs the old age of Manuel, and the threat of it pursues most of the other characters, all of whom ultimately evade it by one means or another.

All of this is to say that while Cabell shares some of the underlying assumptions of the naturalists, he declines to accept their conclusions. He declines to consider man either as merely a transmitter of the life force or as merely a social phenomenon. Moreover, while he grants that humanistic values and ideals are not rooted in reality, that they are illusions or fictions, he declines to give them up; he declines to give up the world of the imagination in favor of "a surrender to life" which leads at one extreme to the primitivistic worship of force and at the other to the complacent acceptance of things as they are.

If Edward Lueders is correct in his analysis of the temper of the twenties, then Cabell's refusal to surrender is one of the things which sets him apart despite the elements of disillusionment and iconoclasm in his writing. In *Carl Van Vechten and the Twenties* Lueders states: "Mabel Dodge Luhan has expressed, in what she recollects of her 'only philosophy in those days,' the fatalistic basis of this creed [of the twenties]: 'Let it happen. Let it decide. Let the great force behind the scenes direct the action. Have faith in life and do not hamper it or try to shape it.'" It should be added that this surrender seems often to have been less an act of faith than an act of desperation full of reluctance and pain.

Cabell sought, instead of such a surrender, a compromise between idealism and naturalism. The solution which he found allies him with those who, in Joseph Wood Krutch's words, "have argued that the way of salvation lay in a sort of ironic belief, in a determination to act as though one still believed the things that were once held true."[6] Among those who have argued this way Krutch lists, "Bertrand Russell in his popular essay, 'A Free Man's Worship,' Unamuno and Santayana, *passim* throughout their works," and of course, he might have added Hans Vaihinger. Within this group Cabell's strongest affinities are with Vaihinger and, particularly, with Santayana. Cabell shares neither the simple stoicism recommended in Russell's essay nor the tragic vision of Unamuno, but the parallels between Cabell's thought and that of Vaihinger and Santayana are surprisingly numerous and fundamental. Vaihinger, Santayana, and Cabell are basically agreed that, "Intellectual morality demands of us that in the sphere of reality we shall not cling to vague possibilities, but shall always prefer the greater probability (i.e. in this case, the assumption that there is no 'life after death,' and in general no divine 'world government,'—no moral world order anywhere)." They agree too that, "It is an error to suppose that an absolute truth, an absolute criterion of knowledge and behavior, can be discovered. The higher aspects of life are based upon noble delusions." They do not, however, for this reason repudiate the higher aspects of life; for them the "value of reality is reversed. . . . The ideal, the unreal is the most valuable."[7] Thus, when Smire faces the specters of naturalism on the banks of the river Styx, he has an answer for their jeering: "Whereafter the nine spectres all screeched together, with their laughter, saying—

"'Now, but this absurd out-of-date creature is telling us, yet again, that the dream is better than the reality!'

"He said then: 'To the contrary, I am telling you that for human kind the dream is the one true reality.' "[8] Santayana, also, has often spoken to the same point: ". . . in *Interpretation of Poetry and Religion* . . . I freely referred to ideals, insisting that Platonic ideas and the deities and dogmas of religion were ideal only: that is to say, they were fictions inspired by the moral imagination. . . . Ideals belonged to poetry, not to science and to serious hypothesis. They were better than any probable or known truth. Far from being less interested in them than if I had thought them true, I was more keenly and humanly interested, for I found them essentially poetical and beautiful, as mere facts are not likely to be."[9]

In his philosophical treatise Vaihinger argues that all the categories of human knowledge rest upon fictions—mental constructions that have no demonstrable relationship to reality; this, he argues, is as true of science and of mathematics as it is of aesthetics and ethics. These fictions are a means of talking about and dealing with reality; in all probability they do not express reality, and therefore their value consists not in their truth but in their fruitfulness. This is a belief which Cabell and Santayana share with Vaihinger, though they are far less interested in scientific and mathematical fictions than in those fictions which determine man's concept of himself and thereby dominate his actions and attitudes. These are the fictions which Cabell calls dynamic illusions—dynamic in that they call forth values and gestures and aspirations that man would not know in their absence.[10]

Cabell further agrees with Vaihinger and with Santayana on the ultimate tendency of these illusions or fictions. What Cabell calls demiurge—that force which shapes the dynamic illusions within man's mind—Vaihinger calls the psyche and Santayana calls spirit. There is, however, this difference: for Vaihinger the psyche seems to be simply identical with mind; for Cabell and for Santayana demiurge or spirit is deeply rooted in the elemental and primitive. It is the product and expression of the obscure principle of animal life "going on very persistently and laboriously in the dark," an animal life which desires only to seize its appropriate prey, to avoid its enemies, and to preserve and propagate itself in safety. In *Beyond Life* Cabell stresses the sex drive as the basic source of energy by means of which dynamic illusions are brought forth and sustained. His awareness that dynamic illusions are from one point of view expressions of primitive animal needs is of considerable importance when we come to consider the theory and techniques of his comedy. In any event, "The fictive activity of the mind is an expression of the fundamental psychical forces; *fictions* are *mental structures*. The psyche weaves this aid to thought out of itself; for the mind is inventive; under the compulsion of necessity, stimulated by the outer world, it discovers the store of contrivances that lie hidden within itself."[11]

This fictive activity, once it has been called into existence, would be totally irresponsible if it were not for the fact that it remains for the most part obedient to the psyche that produced it. "Nothing could be madder, more irresponsible, more dangerous than this guidance of men by dreams. What saves us is the fact that our imaginations, groundless and chimerical as they may seem, are secretly suggested and controlled by shrewd old instincts of our animal nature and by continual contact with things."[12] Cabell, for his part, creates characters—Aesred, Sereda, Maya—to personify these counterbalancing influences. Under the control of our animal natures the fictive activity—or as Cabell would have it, demiurgic activity—creates out of the materials of the senses a coherent and interpretable world picture, and out of the need of the animal to feel at home in the universe, to feel purposeful and independent of the life of nature which threatens it with eternal flux, it creates the world of the ideal.[13] So it comes about that "an ape reft of his tail and grown rusty at climbing" comes to chatter to himself of his "divine paternity" and to feel "himself to be the symbol and the frail representative of omnipotence in a place that is not home. . . ."[14]

Thus, man exists within the subjective envelope of his dreams. "No man lives in the external truth, among salts and acids, among buying and selling, nor amid any doings outside his own skull, and so, to look at any man with mere rationality is but to court deception; it is as though you would measure strong, sound wine with a yardstick . . . for in the warm phantasmagoric chamber of his brain lives every man vaingloriously, among the painted walls and the storied windows."[15] These dreams (fictions, illusions) from the basically humanistic point of view of Cabell, Santayana, and Vaihinger form another more important and equally real dimension of human living. Santayana in explicating what he means by materialism has stated, "that matter is capable of eliciting thought and feeling follows necessarily from the principle that matter is the only *substance, power* or *agency* in the universe; and this, *not* that matter is the only *reality,* is the first principle of materialism." Man's idealized concept, then, of himself and of his place in the scheme of things is not *true* because it has no referent in the material world; but the illusions of which it is composed are *real* in that they exist as ideals and exercise a distinct influence upon man's life.

What is uniquely human in man is his tendency "to play the ape to his dream," to hypostatize his ideals and then attempt to shape his life to their requirements.[16] The result is that man lives in two worlds at once, one of which—what Cabell calls the world of external truths—he can only guess at and which he would not face even if he could. He resolutely refuses to accept the destructive knowledge of Pan: he refuses to accept the naturalistic vision of himself and of his place in the scheme of things.[17] Cabell, Santayana, and Vaihinger have all applauded this refusal. For while it exposes man to the discomforts of disillusionment and the sense of ultimate failure, it also preserves man's humanity. Whatever is courageous or heroic or beautiful in man's life is called out in response to the ideal. To encounter Pan, to throw off all illusions, would be not only to lose all humanistic values but to suffer mental annihilation.

Man is not likely, however, at any given moment to be despoiled of all his illusions. Ordinarily man clings, at the very minimum, to an irrational belief in the efficacy and purposefulness of his immediate activities, of practical work. Taken individually, of course, any illusion is susceptible to detection. "There is indeed no idol ever identified with the ideal which honest experience, even without cynicism, will not some day unmask and discredit. Every real object must cease to be what it seemed, and none could ever be what the whole soul desired."[18] A series of such unmaskings forms the basic stuff of Cabellian comedy, and according to Cabell all men to some extent participate in this process of disillusionment as they fall in love with a being more or less ideal and find themselves married after all to a perfectly human woman. Yet the demiurge is extremely fertile in disguises and in the devices of evasion; it is as patient and resourceful as the spider, and before one web is torn it is already patiently spinning another. The high-hearted idealism of youth slips insensibly into the domesticated urbanity of middle age, and most men come at last, like Gerald Musgrave, to live in reasonable comfort upon Mispec Moor under the care of Maya of the Fair Breasts. Through these fluctuations and revisions of the spirit, man is sustained, as he is sustained in the face of an irrational universe, by his vanity and, perhaps even more so, by his dullness, by his natural "insensibility and by a sort of pervasive immunity to most of the vibrations that run through him."[19]

Both the instability of specific illusions and the seemingly inexhaustible fertility of the demiurge are amply demonstrated in the history of culture than in the phenomenology of spirit. . . . I templation of history should underlie or at least stand near the beginning of Santayana's thought and of Cabell's. Santayana and Cabell have both been deeply interested in human history—not in the history of wars, institutions, and political maneuvers, but in the history of ideals (illusions, fictions) and the concomitant attitudes. What H. M. Rosenthal has observed about Santayana might equally well be applied to Cabell: "I might suggest that Santayana in his comments on historical religion has really been less interested in the history of culture than in the phenomenology of spirit. . . . I mean that he likes to characterize and appraise different dispositions toward the world, in a manner that reminds me of the transcendentalists' interest in attitudes."[20]

Cabell, too, "likes to characterize and appraise different dispositions toward the world"; this is, in fact, one of the main purposes of *Beyond Life* and the ground work of the whole *Biography of Manuel*. Of the many possible dispositions or attitudes, Cabell selects three as being fundamental and historically important, and the rise and decay and blendings and transformations of these form the main streams of the Biography. The three are the chivalric, the gallant, and the poetic. The chivalric attitude, as Cabell defines it, is based upon belief in man's divine parentage and in man's mission as his Father's representative on earth. The gallant attitude is basically skeptical: "The gallant person is a well-balanced skeptic, who comprehends that he knows very little, and probably amounts to somewhat less, but has the grace to keep his temper." The essence of gallantry is "to accept the pleasures of life leisurely, and its inconveniences with a shrug." In short, gallantry is a form of hedonism. The poetic attitude is characterized by the detachment of the artist who accepts the fragmentary and inchoate substance of life, his own life included, merely as raw materials from which he attempts to shape something complete, something symmetrical, satisfying, and enduring.[21] There is also a fourth attitude which is timeless but which Cabell does not elaborate, though obviously he is aware of its importance: the so-called realistic or practical attitude which rests upon the assumption that profitable and productive work, as the world understands these terms, is the proper business of mankind, and which leads to a minimized concern with ends and an exaggerated respect for instrumentalities or means.[22]

Though historically these modes of thought and feeling change—for example, historically both gallantry and chivalry have enjoyed periods of ascendancy—and one attitude with its supporting illusions (ideals, fictions) loses its hegemony and is superseded by another, neither Cabell nor Santayana finds in this movement the signs of essential human progress, but only of succession. "Even if the sequence of ideas in history might be called dialectical, in the sense that no prevalent idea is stable but slips according to the suggestion of the moment into a somewhat different idea, yet this instability presupposes neither logical implication nor moral advance."[23] It is true, of course, that the assumption that all illusions, however complex and apparently remote from animal needs, are nonetheless rooted in natural passions does imply a kind of progress. According to Santayana, the purpose of his *Life of Reason* was "to show how natural passions are fertile in moral principles";[24] a similar purpose may be assigned to Cabell's *Beyond Life;* and from a humanistic point of view, insofar as principles are produced and come to predominate over passions, there is advance. Such advance as is implied in this, however, belongs largely to pre-human history; moreover, both Cabell and Santayana maintain that the instinctive animal life of man persists under the surface, essentially unchanged. As for the illusions (ideals, fictions) themselves, they cannot be realized in the material universe, and therefore they lead to the impossible; the pursuit of any and all of them must end in failure.

This is not to say that illusions are all equally valuable or equally valueless. The value of any given illusion is the measure of its power even momentarily to harmonize and satisfy the demands of human nature and to evoke the fullest possible expression of human potentialities. For this reason Cabell values the ideals of gallantry and chivalry, and Santayana values the ideals of Hellas; and for the same reason Santayana is contemptuous of "the sturdy deformity of the practical mind," and Cabell dislikes common sense and patriotism and piety. These are dynamic illusions like the rest; but their scope is narrow and provincial. From Cabell's point of view they confine and warp the spirit; they thrive upon denial rather than satisfaction, and upon exclusion rather than harmony. Instead of making men "citizens by anticipation of the world we crave," they make men prisoners of an emotionally and spiritually impoverished world.

This method of evaluation is of course pragmatic, but it is pragmatism freed of the usual emphasis upon practicality and success. In this view it is no argument against an illusion (ideal, fiction) that it leads to the impossible, for its value is not dependent upon its realization but upon the transient wayside pleasures and satisfactions that it gives the human spirit. "Everything that satisfies at all, even if partially and for an instant, justifies aspiration and rewards it."[25]

Thus, though the sequence of ideas and ideals in history does not imply progress, it is possible to assign greater or lesser value to individual ideas or ideals. *The Biography of Manuel* is, among many other things, an illustration of this view of history; on one level it may be read as a critique of the idea of progress. In fact, if one reads consecutively through all of the volumes of the Biography, he is likely to come away with the impression that Cabell believed that the quality of human living and character has deteriorated since the thirteenth century. In part this impression is due to fortuitous circumstances. As it happens, in the final form of the

Biography some of Cabell's most mature and powerful works stand close to the beginning. Moreover, if Rudolph Musgrave, Robert Townsend, and Felix Kennaston seem a good deal less imposing than their ancestors in Poictesme, it is partly because they are not seen through the transfiguring mists of time. Still, the impression of decline and deterioration is not purely accidental. The contemporary characters of the Biography live in a scientifically oriented world which allows little scope for the play of the imagination and which is destructive of the larger, bolder illusions; consequently, not only have their lives not been subjected to the myth-making imagination, but they themselves have lost the power of believing in any but relatively mundane illusions. If Rudolph Musgrave's chivalry is timid and stiff-necked, it is because the roots of faith which once nourished the chivalric attitude have been cut away. If Felix Kennaston is a less vigorous character than Jurgen, it is not merely because he is of a different temperament and the product of a less mature creative imagination, but because he is far more self-conscious. Initially Jurgen, for all his skepticism, makes no distinction between a real and an ideal world; he lives in one world, which is a world of unlimited possibilities. Kennaston, on the other hand, is conscious from the beginning of living in a restricted world from which he *escapes* into a world of dreams, of ideal possibilities. Moreover, he is not able to achieve the other world without the aid of the bogus Sigil of Scoteia.

The world-view presented in this chapter is clearly the product of a skeptical mind far gone in disillusionment; that is, a mind no longer capable of a whole-hearted act of faith, no longer able to give unquestioning allegiance to any particular ideal or concept. Skepticism, of course, cannot be absolute; even though the skeptic in theory holds everything in question, animal faith persists within him, and consequently, except when engaged in a deliberate act of criticism, the skeptic, like all men, accepts his world as it appears to him, morally and dramatically. Yet, skepticism does nonetheless destroy the power of conscious belief, and while skeptical minds such as those of Cabell, Vaihinger, and Santayana may be aware that men need their ideals and myths (metaphysical and ethical fictions), they cannot themselves know the satisfaction of believing in these ideals and myths. For them there must be some other solution, some way of approaching the world of the ideal other than that opened by irrational belief.

The attitude which Santayana has called modernism is one such approach: "Modernism is an ambiguous and unstable thing. It is the love of all Christianity in those who perceive that it is all a fable. It is the historic attachment to his church of a Catholic who has discovered that he is a pagan."[26] It is, in other words, a delicate equilibrium wrought by the intellect which allows one simultaneously to perceive that ideals and religious concepts are from a scientific point of view merely fabulous, and yet to value them for their poetic power, that is, their power of evocation and harmonization and their power to make us by anticipation citizens of a better world. This, in general, is what Vaihinger recommends. "We should create for ourselves in imagination a fairer and more perfect world . . . and thereby idealize life. If this principle is once conceded, we shall be compelled to allow its value to myth—as myth. Even the unbeliever . . . can . . . in this sense make the ideal image of Christ his own." And again: "Men must demand the impossible," even if it leads to contradiction." That is, men should behave *as if* the ideal constructions of religion and philosophy were true. As for Cabell, something very like the modernism defined here pervades all of his works; it is the appropriate attitude ultimately discovered by Jurgen, Florian de Puysange, and Felix Kennaston, and it forms the basis of Cabell's explanation of his own adherence to Episcopalianism.

Unfortunately, modernism is, as Santayana points out, unstable. It is a purely intellectual thing, and as such is easily victimized by shifting moods. It remains tenable only so long as certain human sentiments—for instance, the passion for continued existence and for success and realization—are excluded. If these assert themselves strongly enough, modernism is likely to collapse before an overwhelming sense of the hollowness and futility of existence.

There is, however, another possible approach to the ideal, which is perhaps merely a refinement upon modernism. For Santayana this is the way of the philosopher; for Cabell it is the way of the creative artist in the moment of creation. It involves assuming what

Santayana calls a spiritual point of view; that is, assuming an attitude of detachment, "an ironic emancipation from the world and a contempt for it in favor of an 'imaginative play with the non-existent,' a free roaming among whatever essences may swim into the spirit's ken."[28] This concept closely parallels Cabell's concept of the artist who views life from an abnormal height, who in the moment of creation "is uplift a great way beyond mankind: he regards that lesser race with affability, with divine derision, and with complete understanding, in the while that he embalms, forever, his pick of them in the miraculous spicery of his picked words."[29] Moreover, the artist, according to Cabell, in the act of creation is engaged in "playing with ideas"; it isn't belief or disbelief in these ideas which primarily concerns him, but rather their aesthetic possibilities. Thus, his activity is, in Santayana's sense of the word, "spiritual." Cabell argues along with Santayana that the artist in his labors is "irresponsible, technical and visionary," but the upshot of the artist's play is that he seconds the work of the demiurge, and thus, "The human maker of fiction furnishes yet other alcoves, whether with beautiful or shocking ideas, with many fancy-clutching toys that may divert the traveller's mind from dwelling on the tedium of the journey and on the ambiguity of its end."[30] In this way the writer makes it possible for the reader to join him temporarily in the "life of the spirit."

The advantage of the spiritual point of view, or attitude, lies in the fact that it involves no deep emotional commitment to any particular concept within the realm of the ideal; moreover, the pleasure which it elicits from the realm of the ideal is aesthetic and contemplative and not in any way dependent upon realization. It demands neither that the ideal become substance nor that it serve as a source of moral or psychic energy, and therefore it does not carry with it the marked liability to reaction and frustration.

Obviously the spiritual point of view cannot yield a complete *modus vivendi*. It can, however, deeply influence and qualify the response to life, and it is for this very reason that it is, so far as this present study is concerned, an extremely important part of Cabell's world-view. The spiritual point of view plus a certain wholeness of perception which balances the absurdities with the exigencies of life, the losses with the gains, underlies and makes possible Cabell's comic vision.

To summarize Cabell's world-view briefly—man is "just a very gullible consciousness existing among inexplicable mysteries."[31] Nowhere does he touch permanence or immutability; nowhere does he come into direct contact with reality. But insofar as he can guess, with the aid of his reason and his science, the nature of reality, he finds it uncongenial. He finds himself in a universe devoid of moral or rational order, a universe which gives no support to his idealized concept of himself or of his place in the scheme of things and affords no opportunity for the realization of his dreams and aspirations. The ideal goals which he pursues and the world of moral and aesthetic values in which he believes he lives, all these in the perspective of this half-guessed-at reality, prove to be illusions. These illusions, however, are not entirely free-floating fantasies. They are rooted in animal passion and in animal necessity; they are surreptitiously controlled and utilized by the primitive psyche which persists beneath rationality and which is concerned only with the pursuit of its prey, the avoidance of its enemies, and the continuity and propagation of its own existence.

Thus, man lives perforce in two worlds: an ideal world of illusion and a real world. He is, however, protected by his dullness, his innate insensitivity, and by his vanity from ever becoming fully aware of his true condition; and he shows a kind of instinctive wisdom in clinging with irrational tenacity to his groundless beliefs. For these at least are necessary to his sanity and at most make it possible for him to live by anticipation in a better world. Though they lead to contradiction and failure, they do temporarily give direction and purpose to life and do bring momentarily to fruition the finest potential of human nature.

For these reasons even the disillusioned skeptic is wise to make a conscious commitment to the myths and illusions of mankind. Above and beyond this it is possible from time to time and for a short while to join the artist in his free play with ideas, to accept the experience which the artist has prepared for us as a means of exploring the aesthetic possibilities of these ideas.

The Comic Vision

A world-view such as Cabell's may underlie a variety of possible attitudes toward existence. It may issue in the mournful "all is vanity" of Ecclesiastes, in the somewhat brittle stoicism of Russell's "A Free Man's Worship," or in the tragic vision of Miguel de Unamuno. Of all the possibilities, the comic vision seems on first consideration the least likely. The human apprehension of ultimate failure, the ego's abhorrence of being duped, and its passion for security and continuity—all these are strong affections which are excited or threatened by this view, and, as Freud has argued, aroused affections are inevitably hostile to the comic spirit.[1]

If these elemental passions and needs assert themselves vigorously enough, the threatened psyche can only respond with a cry of pain, and the result, at least for the literary artist, is the tragic vision. This, for instance, is precisely the case with Miguel de Unamuno, who shares with Cabell and with Santayana so many assumptions about the ultimate nature of reality. He could not accept without pain the dependence of spirit upon matter: "I cannot resign myself to one day returning to unconsciousness, because I have a thirst for eternity. . . . That a man should not believe in another life, that I understand, for I myself find no proof of it; but that he should resign himself to this, and above all that he should not desire anything more than this life, that is a thing that I do indeed not understand." Nor could he either come to terms with or be satisfied personally to evade Aesred, the goddess of common sense and compromise, whom he confronts under the name of Antonia Quixano.[2] He must revolt and kick against the pricks of reality. "Paraphrasing a passage in Senancour's *Obermann,* he [Unamuno] reaches his form of the categorical imperative: 'Let us act so that the nothing becomes an injustice. Let us battle against destiny even if there is no hope of victory. Let us battle against it quixotically.' "[3] Thus, life becomes a series of injustices, and death the greatest injustice of all; man is caught in a web of injustices and he is led into painful and futile combat by what is finest in him. This essentially is the tragic vision of Unamuno.

Unamuno's vision is so thoroughly consistent with the logic of human nature that, given his world-view, it seems almost inevitable; yet neither Cabell nor Santayana share it, though they start with the same root concepts. Essentially Cabell agrees with Santayana that "everything in nature is lyrical in its ideal essence, tragic in its fate, and comic in its existence."[4] That nature is lyrical in its ideal essence needs no further discussion here, if we understand lyrical to refer to that which is shaped and directed by emotion and desire rather than by observation and reason. That it is tragic in its fate Cabell accepts with reservations: "Really there is a thin sustenance for the tragic muse in the fact that with each performance [of the human comedy] the flesh-and-blood costume is spoiled. . . ."[5] It is this concession that largely accounts for the vagrant note of pathos that plays through his works. But for the most part Cabell chooses to dwell upon the comic of existence; he prefers, as he says in the Preface to "The Lineage of Lichfield," the "comedic metaphor": man conceived of as "itinerant comedian." Like one of his own creations, Smire, who is after all for Cabell a sort of imaginary alter ego, Cabell has found a never-failing source of amusement in mankind's "inexhaustible foolishness."[6] "Yet do these tiny and trite comedies amuse you [Cabell himself] as though they were performed for the first time. You find in small human follies an unfailing zest. When the inane pester you, then you play at anger, unavailingly: your brows frown but beneath them your lips are smiling at the droll ways of men and women."[7] Moreover, it is not merely the foolishness and inanities of human existence that are comic. From Cabell's point of view, though he disclaims any knowledge of the plot of the universal drama, one thing is certain— insofar as man strives to exceed the very severe limitations which material nature imposes upon him, he casts himself in the role of fool.[8] Thus, the comic is inherent in every pattern of human living which departs from the purely sentient and instinctive.

The key to this opposition between Unamuno's tragic vision and Cabell's comic vision, growing though they do out of the same intellectual soil, is the relatively greater detachment of Cabell as against the passionate personal involvement of Unamuno. Unamuno conceives of himself, and so of the literary artist, as "wrestling with God from morning till night," as leading an impassioned though futile revolt against the life-denying forces of reason and science.[9] Cabell, on the other hand, conceives of the literary artist, and thus of himself, as, in the moment of creation, "uplift a great way beyond mankind," from which vantage point "he regards that lesser race with affability, with divine derision, and with complete understanding."[10] From this god-like eminence, the artist has a simultaneous vision of "is and seems," and because he is freed from a sense of personal involvement, he is free to respond to the incongruities of existence as comic rather than shocking or painful.

Perhaps this can be further clarified by again referring to the philosophy of Santayana. As was pointed out in the preceding chapter, Cabell's concept of the perspective of the artist corresponds closely to Santayana's concept of the perspective of spirit. Spirit in Santayana's definition is a natural entelechy, a perfection of function, that function being the intuition of essences (illusions, fictions); spirit arises out of the need of the psyche to perceive the world through which it moves; consequently, the essences which spirit reports are given moral color.[11] The tendency of spirit is, however, toward a free and irresponsible roaming among essences. If spirit were entirely free from the pressures of animal existence, it would find its fulfillment in the joyful contemplation of whatever essences presented themselves to it. Accordingly as a man becomes more spiritual, as Santayana defines the term, he approaches a total dis-intoxication from animal interests and values.[12]

Though pure spirit would never discover anything but essences and would be completely content to dally with these, a man of spiritual mind, using the vantage point of spirit for the purpose of making a critical survey of life, perceives not only that essences (illusions, fictions) have only poetic value but also that existence is inherently comic. For he perceives that man, who assumes sta-bility, lives actually in the midst of flux: "Existence involves changes and happenings and is comic inherently like a pun that begins with one meaning and ends with another. Incongruity is a consequence of change; and this incongruity becomes especially noticeable when, as in the flux of nature, change is going on at different rates in different strands of being, so that not only does each thing surprise itself by what it becomes, but it is continually astonished and dis-concerted, by what other things have turned into without its leave."[13] Or to paraphrase this in Cabellian terms—youth, with all its high-flown and romantic pursuit of the ideal, is metamorphosed by such insensible degrees into something else utterly different from what it was that by and by a man comes to stand bewildered by his inability to recognize his own image in the glass; and at the same time he finds himself in possession of and possessed by innumerable things which he never consciously sought and which seem to have come into his life like changelings undetected.

Moreover, a man of spiritual mind perceives that essences con-ceal and serve a reality quite different from the one they seem to announce and that when they are accepted as the basis for action or belief, they lead to contradiction and to impossible postures and presumptions. He sees that the world is constantly in imminent danger of being unmasked, and, in fact, the act of perception is itself a kind of unmasking. In short, "The world is a perpetual caricature of itself; at every moment it is a mockery and contradic-tion of what it is pretending to be. But as it nevertheless intends all the time to be something different and highly dignified, at the next moment it corrects and checks and tries to cover up the absurd thing that it was; so that a conventional world, a world of masks, is superimposed upon the reality, and passes in every sphere of human interest for the reality itself."[14] Or again to paraphrase in Cabellian terms—man is doomed by his inadequate flesh to parody his dreams, and, as John Charteris contends in *Beyond Life*, "the accepted routine of life's conduct tends to make mountebanks of us inevitably: and the laborious years weave small hypocrisies like cobwebs about our every action and at last about our every thought."[15]

Considering the demonstrated parallels and similarities between Cabell's world-view and Santayana's, and between Cabell's notion of the viewpoint of the artist and Santayana's concept of the viewpoint of the spiritual mind, there is surely no impossible inductive leap involved in substituting artist for spiritual mind in the preceding comments. Even the language which Cabell and Santayana use in describing the qualities of these respective attitudes, is parallel. Where Cabell speaks of "affability" and "divine derision," Santayana speaks of "tolerance" and "irony."

What the artist perceives, then, from his private Olympus is that life is a congeries of incongruities and contradictions, that existence is forever susceptible to being unmasked and that everywhere one is confronted with disjunctions between ends and means and with disappointed expectations; in other words, he finds that life is replete with the crude matter of comedy. As has been said, these surprises and disappointments, if they are, so to speak, experienced from within, produce shock and pain; but given detachment or disintoxication, they issue in a comic vision of life. Detachment, it should be understood, does not rule out the possibility of affection or even of love. The antics of a child mimicking the manners and gestures of adults are generally comic because of the incongruity between object and representation; and the parent, who genuinely loves the child, has no difficulty in reconciling his detached appreciation of these comic roles with his continuing love for the actor. Significantly Cabell's image of the artist is not only god-like but paternal; for him affability and tenderness, if not love, are essential concomitants of the artist's perspective and of his vision.

It is this detached or disintoxicated viewpoint that has made possible Cabell's comic vision, that has made it possible for him, in Ellen Glasgow's words, "to look into the abyss and laugh."[16] Of course, a comic vision of life is not synonymous with comedy. A comic vision may lead to nothing more than a predisposition to laugh at life; comedy, on the other hand, is an art form; that is, it is an artificial structure more or less self-consciously designed to fulfill a special function, specifically in this case to convey the comic vision and its attendant benefits. Presumably, when Cabell subtitled many of his books "comedies," he was aware of this distinction; therefore, we must next turn to a consideration of the nature of comedy with the ultimate purpose of defining Cabellian comedy.

The Theory of Comedy

Though there appears to be great divergence of opinion among the commentators on the nature of comedy, when their works are compared it quickly becomes apparent that in many points they agree; and though the areas of disagreement involve such fundamental matters as the function of comedy, the possibilities proposed are not numerous. They can be classified under two or three headings.

There is no disagreement about the *immediate* effect sought in comedy; that is, the arousing of comic laughter or at least of a smile which may be considered as tentative laughter. There is also general agreement that comedy, in contrast to tragedy, presents typical situations or, in Albert Cook's terms, deals with the probable, and that the characters of comedy are either types or individuals who can be readily classified as types. Molière's Alcestis, for example, strikes us as an individual; yet, he is readily classified as "the misanthrope." By contrast, the tragic protagonist is unique; he creates a new category into which others may fall. Consider Oedipus and Hamlet. Commentators since and including Bergson have also generally agreed that, at least initially, the attitude aroused by comedy is similar to the play attitude: an attitude which leads one to conceive of himself and of the characters of the comedy as playing roles. Under these circumstances one is not predisposed to take the action of the comedy seriously, in the sense of sharing the emotions of the character and of identifying one's interests with those of the protagonist. In general, comedy avoids stimulating strong affections, for these are hostile to comic laughter. Moreover—and here again there is general agreement—comedy views life from a social point of view and is concerned with man primarily as a social being.

Comedy, then, provides an overtly artificial experience designed to arouse comic laughter through the observance of types of humanity as seen from a social point of view. Thus far there is agreement. There is agreement too that comedy affirms the possibilities of life and ends happily, at least from the spectator's or reader's point of view.

Disagreement, however, becomes sharp and irreconcilable when the question of function or the closely related question of the source of comic laughter is raised. There is a broad general assumption that the function of comedy is ultimately social, but the exact nature of this social function is debated. Basically, the various theories of the function of comedy may be classified under, at most, three headings: the corrective-reformatory, the cathartic, and closely related to the cathartic, the ritual expulsion theory of Albert Cook.

Henri Bergson, George Meredith, and James Feibleman are the chief proponents of the corrective-reformatory theory. Bergson conceives of the comic experience as a purely intellectual experience: "To produce the whole of its effect . . . the comic demands something like a momentary anesthesia of the heart. Its appeal is to the intelligence, pure and simple." The function of comedy for him is the correction of any rigidity or inelasticity in men and their affairs, or, stated conversely, comedy strives to produce a maximum of elasticity and sociability: "The comic is that side of a person which reveals his likeness to a thing, that aspect of human events, which, through its peculiar inelasticity, conveys the impression of pure mechanism, of automatism, of movement without life. Consequently it expresses an individual or collective imperfection which calls for an immediate correction. This corrective is laughter, a social gesture that singles out and represses a special kind of absent-mindedness in men and in events." In its personal application the intention of laughter is to humiliate, "to correct our neighbor, if not in his will, at least in his deed."[1] But more generally laughter is a kind of automatic recoil of the mind, a built-in mechanism for protecting society, which requires adaptability, against fossilization in its members or in its institutions. In consonance with this theory of function, Bergson argues that all the sources of comic laughter may be reduced to automatism, to the perception of something inert or mechanical encrusted upon life. In Bergson's view comedy is, then, on the side of progress; for by freeing society from the inert, the ceremonial, the purely mechanical, it helps to prepare the way for future growth.

The English novelist, George Meredith, in his essay "On the Idea of Comedy and the Uses of the Comic Spirit," takes a position which in several respects approximates Bergson's. He, like Bergson, conceives of comedy as a social corrective and argues that the comic experience is a highly civilized and purely intellectual experience. However, he restricts the scope of comedy even more severely than Bergson does. Not only does he exclude humor and satire from the purlieus of comedy but he also limits the legitimate prey of the comic spirit to man's social character: "The comic poet is in the narrow field, or enclosed square, of the society he depicts, and he addresses the still narrower enclosure of men's intellects, with reference to the operation of the social world upon their characters." Moreover, from Meredith's point of view it is not mechanism or automatism that arouses comic laughter, but rather any deformity, disproportion, or malfunction in the social character: "Men's future upon earth does not attract it [the comic spirit]; their honesty and shapeliness in the present does."[2] Nor does Meredith conceive of the corrective function of comedy as being fulfilled in the forthright way proposed by Bergson. Comedy exercises a corrective influence because those who recognize the comic possibilities of social life and character naturally shrink from becoming the object of comic laughter, and this in itself is a step toward refinement. For, according to Meredith, comic laughter is always on the side of common sense and, therefore, of civilization. Comedy, then, in Meredith's view promotes the cultivation of the individual and reinforces the common-sense norms upon which civilization is based. We might call Meredith's theory corrective-normative, and Bergson's corrective-progressive.

One of the grace notes of Meredith's theory is the proposition that comedy is "an exhibition of women's battle with men, and that of men with them." Women, he claims, enjoy an elevated position in comedy because their wit is generally on the side of common sense, and though he does not say so, the implication is that comedy witnesses and promotes the triumph of the feminine spirit over the masculine.[3] This is particularly interesting in view of what we will observe shortly about Cabell's concept of comedy.

Of course, as Joseph Warren Beach has pointed out,[4] Meredith's essay on comedy is an inadequate shadowing forth of his own comic intention, an incomplete formulation of a program rather than an analysis. The impression given by the essay is that Meredith has chiefly in mind the kind of comedy of manners which thrives upon the ridicule of social ineptness and eccentricity; no doubt this impression is at variance with Meredith's practice as a writer of comic narrative. For under Meredith's management the comic spirit is the watchdog of common sense sniffing out those eccentricities of soul which often lie deep buried in the psychological makeup of the protagonist. However, whether we look to the well-known and influential theory—which is our main concern in this chapter—or to the practice in the novels, the fact remains that Meredith is not concerned, as Bergson apparently is, in liberating the forces of progressive evolution. Meredith's civilization is not something which can be defined only as it comes into being; it is of the order of nature and can be defined and practically expressed through the exertion of common sense which is in turn the expression of nature in man. Meredith's civilization is rooted in naturalness of behavior and expression—naturalness being understood somewhat in the normative, eighteenth century sense.

In his book, *In Praise of Comedy*, James Feibleman argues that comedy performs a progressive function, is inherently revolutionary.[5] As might be expected, Feibleman rejects the conservatism and exclusiveness of Meredith's theory which he sees as the consequence of artificial restrictions forced upon Meredith by the genteel tradition. Not quite so expectedly Feibleman also rejects Bergson's theory. Though at first glance Bergson's corrective-progressive theory appears to have strong affinities with Feibleman's, Feibleman rejects it, first because Bergson's metaphysics leads to the assumption that comedy is inimical to the idea of system itself, and secondly, because Bergson's theory, as Feibleman understands it, is ultimately subjective in emphasis. Feibleman insists that comedy does not criticize systems, theories, and customs in the interest of flux (Bergson's assumption) but in the interest of a better system, a more logical and ideal order. Moreover, he insists upon an ontological rather than a psychological or subjective approach to comedy. He does not wholly reject the insights of those who have studied the psychology of laughter, but he insists that the study of comedy must not be restricted to these subjective aspects and that in a completely developed theory of comedy the subjective must be subordinated to the effort to arrive at a realistic definition of comedy. In answer to his own question—what is comedy in itself?—Feibleman concludes that "comedy . . . consists in the indirect affirmation of the ideal logical order by means of the derogation of the limited orders of actuality." The comedian's or the comic writer's standard procedure is to juxtapose what is with what ought to be, and "laughter is the sudden recognition of the wide difference between what is and what ought to be." In the presence of what ought to be, what is appears defective, limited, comic—which is to say, impotent. The net result, then, of the comic experience is liberation from the tyranny of the actual and, consequently, preparation for progress, that is, the realization of a more ideal or logical order. Feibleman admits that comedy may have a romantic or reactionary orientation which locates what ought to be in the past rather than in the future, but he insists, somewhat arbitrarily, that "high" comedy derogates all past and present actuals in favor of some future form.

The cathartic theory of comic function differs from the corrective theory in its insistence that the comic experience is basically emotional rather than intellectual or judicial, and in its subordination of the social to the individual in defining the effects of comedy. From the viewpoint of the cathartic theory, comic laughter acts as "a social prophylactic," not because it castigates or threatens with castigation, but because its effect upon the reader or auditor is that of purgation or harmonization. For example, Lane Cooper in his hypothetical reconstruction of an Aristotelian theory of comedy[6] argues that the immediate purpose of comedy is to arouse comic laughter by the contemplation of disproportion (defectiveness) in men and in things, and thereby to purge our sense of disproportion— injustice and defectiveness—in daily life. In freeing us of our sense of disproportion, comedy frees us of anger and envy which are the emotional by-products of this sense and which are harmful to the community as well as to the individual who harbors them. Thus, the experience of comedy confers upon the spectator or reader "an elevated calm, or tranquility of soul, with a clear mental perspective and freedom from disturbing emotion."

In Cooper's view, comedy may be "a specific for folly," not, however, because, as Meredith thought, it threatens individual social aberrations with castigation, but because it restores the mental and emotional health of those who experience it. Comedy preserves the health of society by preserving the health of its citizens. Moreover, because Cooper is not bound to a theory of comedy as a more or less direct social corrective, he is free to accept a broader base for comic subject matter and comic laughter. Though he states that comedy deals with ordinary citizens in commonplace situations, he argues also that "an element of the marvelous," which is basically illogical or irrational, has a place in comedy. Actually, though the comic character is "one from the number of everyday citizens," Cooper conceives of him as a type either below the average or depressed below the average for comic purposes. Accordingly, he argues that one of the major techniques of comedy is caricature, and that caricature, along with surprise and disappointed expectation, is the main source of comic laughter. Moreover, to Meredith's assertion that the final test of "true comedy" is that it shall "awaken thoughtful laughter," Cooper replies, "The restriction is too narrow. Writers from Aristophanes to Shakespeare and Molière have employed every sort of means to arouse laughter—lofty wit and naughty as well,—tending only to avoid what is painful or corrupting."

Willard Smith is at one with Lane Cooper in rejecting the corrective theory of comedy and in seeing at least part of the effect of comedy as catharsis.[7] First of all he argues that the play attitude, which predominates in the experience of comedy, cancels out the critical, judicial attitude assumed by Meredith and by Bergson. The audience witnessing a comedy (Smith speaks only of drama, but what he says may be applied also to comic narrative) may be judicial in the sense that it is detached and, so to speak, sees all around the actors, but because it is encouraged to think of itself and the actors as at play, it is not inclined to exercise moral or ethical judgment. Consequently, comedy fails as a direct social corrective. Yet, according to Smith, comedy, which normally presents the spectacle of "a man becoming the dupe of his nonconformity to the conventional aspects of the moral law," results in an *unconscious* fortification of the spectator's adherence to social decorum. Moreover, comedy with its attitude of play and its commonsense social point of view "acts as a catharsis upon our over-absorption in self" and thereby readjusts us to the scale of society, harmonizes us with our fellows. Unlike Lane Cooper, however, Smith conceives of the catharsis of comic laughter as less exclusively the purging away of disturbing emotions. "Physiologically what accompanies the emotional release of energy is a preparation of the organism for vigorous action. The released energy is not wasted but redirected . . . by cerebral activity. Laughter so considered is no longer a safety-valve, a mere blowing-off of potentially dangerous nervous energy, but a means of introducing harmony into the individual character of man. Comedy of any kind thus becomes a means of harmonization." The experience of comedy, then, having purged the spectator of his self-consciousness (over-absorption in self) and having wrought a harmonization of his character, leaves him *unconsciously* disposed to "tackle the first moral problem that confronts him, in a manner less personal and more objective."

Closely allied with the cathartic theory of comedy, yet independent and unique in emphasis, is Albert Cook's concept of comedy as ritual expulsion.[8] According to Cook's definition, the perspective of comedy is that of the probable: comedy accepts the norms of probable social experience and ridicules any individualistic deviation from these norms. "The individualist may be equally a drunkard, a satyr, an aristorcrat, a saint, or an artist; in any case, non-social abnormality is expelled from society by laughter. In this sense laughter is superiority, though always the superiority of the group which follows the mean over the abnormal individual whose excess it constrains." The fact that this expulsion is conceived of as *ritual* expulsion underscores the idea that the comic experience does not lead to action but is merely the confirmation of pre-existing attitudes. The normal pattern of comedy is, as Cook describes it, "the abnormality of the pariah, his expulsion by normal society, joy of society." In the instances in which the abnormality of the pariah expresses the spectator's or reader's own secret desires and foibles, the ritual expulsion of comedy provides a purgation of guilt which, paradoxically, may readily result in a renewed will to sin. All in all, in the light of Cook's theory, comedy emerges as conservative or even reactionary in function rather than progressive.

Both Feibleman and Cook, though they are divergent in practically every other respect, recognize the existence of more than one kind of comedy, and each singles out for special treatment a particular form of comedy which is in fact an extreme modification of the basic comic pattern as they conceive it. Feibleman talks of "divine comedy"; Cook talks of "serene comedy." Divine comedy is, according to Feibleman, like other comedy, critical of actuality, but its criticism is more diffuse. For divine comedy takes as its subject the totality of the "finite predicament" and discovers a logic in actual events which implies that the actual serves or is groping toward the ideal. Moreover, divine comedy enters into the private perspective and discovers that public failure is often private success and vice versa. The obvious example of this sort of comedy is Dante's *Divine Comedy.*' Serene comedy differs from normal comedy in that it treats of the wonderful (in Cook's theory the appropriate subject matter of tragedy) and reverses the normal comic pattern. Instead of building up to the expulsion of the pariah, it begins with "the expulsion of the self-searcher," continues with his adventures in the wonderful, and ends with "his rehabilitation with new knowledge into the control of society." The main examples of this sort of comedy are the *Odyssey* and *The Tempest.*

Both divine comedy and serene comedy, as presented by their

respective analysts, encroach upon the domain of tragedy—divine comedy by abandoning the social perspective for a perspective that is simultaneously personal and cosmic; serene comedy by subsuming the realm of the wonderful—and both make a near approach to the function of tragedy.

This rather lengthy preamble in the form of a survey of the various theories of comedy is not designed to provide a pigeonhole or pigeonholes into which Cabell's idea of comedy can be fitted, nor is there any intention of trying to reconcile contradictory views or to decide relative merits. Rather, the purpose of the survey is to provide a background against which Cabell's ideas may be more clearly and efficiently defined.

From what has been said about Cabell's world-view, it should be fairly obvious that, whatever his idea of comedy may be, he is not likely to look to comedy as a corrective in either Bergson's sense or Meredith's. For Cabell flux is merely the necessary and inevitable condition of the comedy of existence; it is not, as for Bergson, a positive good. From Cabell's point of view comedy may be said to *capitalize* upon flux but hardly to function in its interest. For Cabell finds no assured promise of progressive evolution in the flux of nature, no assurance that the stream of time flows toward the new Jerusalem, and flux in relation to the individual human life is morally ambiguous, being simultaneously good and evil according to the point of view assumed.

As for the fear of becoming the object of comic laughter, a fear upon which Meredith bases his belief in the corrective effect of comedy—Cabell's point of view affords it little weight. Only in the narrow social perspective of Meredith's theory, which accepts the norms and values of common-sense civilization as good if not abso-lute, can such be seen as salutary. In the more or less cosmic perspective of Cabellian comedy, the alternative to folly is less attractive. Man may play the fool, or he may accept his limitations, sacrificing to common sense and routine all of his dreams and aspira-tions, and living in consequence a stunted, narrow life.[10] Moreover, even if he chooses to make this sacrifice, he cannot hope to escape being the cat's-paw of the ironist, for he merely exchanges one set of illusions for another. In the end Queen Stultitia of Philistia and her adherents are as much the objects of irony and of comic laughter as Jurgen and Manuel ever are. Furthermore, the self-consciousness which Meredith counts upon to restrain men within the bounds of common sense suggests to Cabell quite other possibilities. As he views the matter, self-consciousness opens the possibility of self-appreciation and applause, and so may encourage rather than dissuade man from his ancient comic routine.[11]

Whereas for Meredith the comic *arises* when man, measured by the common-sense norms, grows disproportionate, for Cabell, as we have seen, the comic is immanent in all existence; it is a dye that stains the web of existence through and through. The perception of this comic aspect of all actuality is a matter of finding the proper perspective. Such a view quite naturally leads to a liberalization of Meredith's theory of the proper mode and subject matter of comedy. The comic artist has all times and all human experience and all human concepts to play with. He is no longer confined to the "enclosed square of his own society," nor is the means by which he arouses comic laughter any longer restricted by conceptions of cultivation and decorum. As a matter of practice Cabell does not shun any of the many techniques for arousing comic laughter. To shun any particular comic mode or form is after all to miss part of the comedy of existence.

Far from enlisting comedy exclusively in the service of common sense, Cabell conceives one of the possible, legitimate functions of all literature to be the vicarious evasion or breaking of taboos. In discussing the significance of the rogue character in literature, Cabell states: "Everywhere, in fine, this or that pleasant action is forbidden or in one way or another restricted; and man, upon the verge of actual, sharp, zestful enjoyment, is brought up short by a taboo of his own invention." The appeal of the rogue—for example, of Tyl Ulenspiegel—is that he, according to Cabell, offers the reader an opportunity to escape momentarily from his inhibitions and repressions. Cabell's extensive use of phallicism and double-entendre and his use of the rogue character may be seen as by-products of this concept, though, as we shall see, in the context of his fully realized theory these devices come to have additional and more fundamental significance.

Here Cabell's thought might seem to parallel Freud's, but Cabell's concept of comedy is not ultimately Freudian. Comedy, for him, is never merely the toppling of taboos. This is not to say, either, that Freud's concept is merely this. Actually Freud does not present a complete theory of comedy. In exploring the psychological bases of the major forms of comic laughter, he depends largely upon jokes and upon what Feibleman calls "informal comedy, accidental humor, accidentally appreciated." The point is, however, that Cabell recognizes some of the same bases and, because of his broader view of the nature of the comic situation, is able to exploit them, to find employment for the comic spirit outside of the rather arbitrary limitations laid down by Meredith and others.

Yet there is a sense in which Cabell may claim service along with Meredith and Molière under the aegis of Aesred, goddess of common sense, compromise, and the wisdom of the middle way. When we probe Cabell's thought deeply enough we fall upon paradoxes which can be resolved only in the light of a synthesis of his thought which he does not make for us. Here we have one such paradox. Cabell claims that the creative writer (the comic writer is, of course, included) "plays with piety": he evades and violates the taboos of society, all of which are sacred to Aesred, and "leads one more desperate sortie from the routine of existence."[12] In other words, the writer raises a revolt against Aesred, the weight and power of whose reign is largely felt in the weight of daily routine and custom. The direction which Cabell's own sorties take is into the realm of fantasy, symbol, and myth. Still, Cabell is not being wholly facetious or ironic when he claims that: "Throughout the last some and twenty years, in the while that my more temerarious fellows have with untiring typewriters assailed and derided her notions, I have written on sedately in praise of monogamy in *Jurgen*, and of keeping up appearances in *Figures of Earth*, and of chastity in *Something about Eve*, and of womanhood in *Domnei*, and of religion in *The Silver Stallion*: and indeed throughout the building of the Biography I have at every instant upheld, in my own unpresuming way, all that Aesred endorses as the more comfortable fetishes for a man to believe in."[13] Insofar as this is ironic, it is ironic because it elaborates a half-truth which implies the other half, but the half-truth stands. The typical Cabell hero—Jurgen, Gerald Musgrave, Florian de Puysange—ultimately does come to terms with actuality and does submit to Aesred.

A similar and closely related paradox is that probed by Granville Hicks' somewhat peevish question—If Cabell believes that men need their illusions, why does he spend all of his time destroying those illusions?[14] William Parker is involved with the same paradox when he finds it bewildering "that while he [Cabell] is praising the efficacy of a dream-denial of reality, he is constantly giving the reader a sense of that reality."[15] Everywhere in his works Cabell insists that man's sanity and survival depend upon certain dynamic illusions which help him to avoid becoming aware of his true situation in the universe. Moreover, Cabell states in more than one place that the function of the creative artist is to second the work of the demiurge by creating yet other attractive illusions, to present things as they "ought to be" and thereby to make available to the reader an ideal world. Yet in practice Cabell does not ever allow the reader to escape for long into a world of illusions; every illusion which enters into Cabell's comedies—whether it be ideal beauty or justice or holiness—is subjected to the searching light of irony, and there is shown to be either substanceless or an all but transparent veil masking an unexpected but quite probable actuality. Thus, the romantic pursuit of ideal beauty, symbolized by the beautiful woman, ends in the embrace of flesh, the begetting of children, and perhaps in marriage.

There is a strong temptation to seize upon one term of these paradoxes and to ignore the other. Having noted the fact that Cabell is an ironist, it is tempting to consider his works simply as satires upon the vanity of human wishes and to concur with Maurice Le Breton's conclusion: "Effleurant tout, sans jamais insister, il dégonfle au passage les vanités, ramène les folies au bon sens, dépouille prestement . . . l'égoïsme humain des voiles de l'hypocrisie, et mettant l'homme à nu pour le punir de son orgueil, il se donne le malin plaisir, pour l'humilier, de le donner en spectacle, l'espace d'un moment, aux dieux ironiques de l'Univers."[16] Seen from this point of view, the pattern of Cabellian comedy, despite Cabell's often repeated pronouncements in favor of the dream-denial of reality, would seem to fit Willard Smith's definition of comedy as the spectacle of "a man becoming the dupe of his own non-conformity." There is a limited truth in this; Jurgen, Florian de Puysange, and Gerald Musgrave are in a certain sense duped by, or at least in spite of, their nonconformity. But nonetheless the definition is too narrow. For a reasonably close reader cannot help becoming aware of what Régis Michaud has pointed out: "Les rêveurs qu'il met en scène finissent, il est vrai, en désappointés. Mais ils n'ont pas l'air de regretter leur voyage et, à la ferveur avec laquelle ils se le rappellent, on sent toujours en eux des songeurs impénitents."[17] The simple formula of the duped and exposed nonconformist will not cover the facts. The Cabellian hero is impenitent, and even more significant, though he may be the dupe of his nonconformity, he is also rewarded by it. If the comedies end with "all is vanity," they also end with "much have I travelled in the realms of gold" and "the mind is its own place."

Moreover, Cabell's most overt and mordant satire is reserved for those who conform too closely, who narrowly restrict the scope of human living in the interest of prudish taboos and the fetish of practicality. In the story of Prospero in *These Restless Heads*, Ariel is presented as something of a fusion of the spirit of romance with the comic spirit out of Meredith. It is not, however, the pariah whom this spirit derides but rather the dull citizens of Milan who are dead to the "winds blowing out of the isles of wonder" and Prospero himself, the apostate artist who has turned practical statesman.[18]

Actually, for all the difficulty which they create, these paradoxes are to a large extent resolvable; the confusion which they occasion arises from a too narrow definition of irony and a too thoroughly conventional notion of disillusionment. For example, when Hicks complains that Cabell destroys the very illusions that in theory he believes desirable, Hicks is apparently assuming that irony destroys its object, or that irony, by attaching value to the opposite of what is apparent or asserted, thereby empties that which is asserted or apparent of *all* value and significance. (Some such concept of irony seems also to underlie the corrective theories of Bergson and Feibleman; for both theorists the perception of an incongruity leads to the complete devaluation of one of the incongruous elements.) This may be true of sarcastic comments and of the familiar inverted comments on the weather, but that it is not necessarily true of more complex and sophisticated irony is readily demonstrated by reference to so well known a work as Swift's *Modest Proposal*. The irony in the Modest Proposal arises initially from the obvious discrepancy between tone and subject matter, and the reader quickly concludes that the speaker must mean the opposite of what he says. Yet, at a deeper—though still ironic—level it is apparent that the proposal is no more cruel than existing practices, and therefore what the speaker says about the modesty and the mercifulness of his proposal acquires a certain validity. At least, if the reader is willing to tolerate existing practices, he has no rational grounds for rejecting the speaker's suggestions as inhuman. The speaker's assertions are simultaneously true and not true depending upon which system of values they are referred to.

In *The First American Gentleman* Cabell himself takes an opportunity to complain of the common misconception about the nature of irony: " 'So why, my dear Luis, do you need to keep on saying the opposite of what you mean, at this hour of the night when we both ought to have been in bed long ago?'

" 'You mistake me, my dove,' returned Don Luis, as he took off his jerkin, and began to unfasten his codpiece resignedly, 'if but because no true-born American has ever ventured to distinguish between the ironist and the idiot.' "[19]

In Marjorie Burke's Introduction to *Quiet, Please*[20] there occurs a passage which is largely valid and supposedly carries Cabell's endorsement. The philosopher of art is speaking: "Irony, as your art well reveals, Mr. Cabell, proves that any assertion is dogmatic and one-sided, and vulnerable to contradiction. *Irony conjures a bipartient vision of reality*, however, and therefore the ironist, I contend, is the only rational artist. With his grasp of *reality's double value*, he alone is able to whittle man down to his proper size and place."

Irony, then, is not a matter of saying the opposite of what is meant; it is a means of saying more than one thing at a time. It exposes the double value of reality—the dream interpretation and the actual. From this point of view (and the point is that this is apparently Cabell's intention) the irony to which Cabell subjects human illusions does not destroy those illusions or drain them of their value; it merely detaches them from the actual. For example, the "beautiful woman" may be said to be a momentary fusion of the ideal and the actual, and for a time the pursuit of her may become identical with the pursuit of ideal beauty, but ultimately it becomes apparent that the fusion is extremely unstable and that the pursuit masks the sex drive of the primitive psyche which finds its satisfaction in physical union. The perception of this is ironic; however, it does not invalidate the concept of ideal beauty or the longing which men experience for it. It merely demonstrates that man participates in more than one realm of being, an ideal-illusory realm and an actual-physical realm, and that only temporary and imaginary conjunctions can exist between these realms. In their own realm these ideals or illusions retain all of their attractiveness and potency—a discovery which, for example, Jurgen shares with Plato and Santayana.

The critical misunderstanding of the function of irony in Cabellian comedy lies at the root of another misunderstanding which is revealed in the generally inappropriate designation of Cabell's comedies as comedies of disillusionment. To call Cabellian comedy a comedy of disillusionment may be useful, provided the term—disillusionment—is carefully defined so that it does not carry the purely conventional connotations. Ordinarily disillusionment is vaguely conceived of as a negative psychological state in which all value is denied, a state leading to cynicism and associated with embitterment. No doubt as a description of disillusionment as a purely emotional experience in the absence of philosophy, this definition may be accurate enough, but how such a state can be fruitfully associated with Cabellian comedy is not clear. Certainly the reader is not left with the sense of either having participated in or having witnessed an embittering experience. Excluding brief moments of pathos, he has been amused by the whole spectacle. As for the comic protagonist—while it is true that he is "disappointed," he is not embittered, he does not regret his voyage into the wonderful. At the end both Jurgen and Gerald Musgrave realize that they have been tricked, and they are momentarily saddened by the knowledge. They are not, however, overwhelmed by it. Very quickly they adapt themselves to their new situation: Jurgen by turning his romantic imagination upon his actual domestic arrangements and Gerald by substituting different and generally more acceptable illusions for those which are no longer accessible to him.

Used in a different sense, however, the word may be meaningfully applied to Cabellian comedy. Disillusionment may be associated with freedom from delusion, delusion being the search for the ideal embodied in the actual. Such freedom is both the source and the gift of the ironic double-vision which perceives simultaneously the limited actual world and the world of ideals (illusions) which man futilely attempts to realize in the actual. It denies neither world; it merely declares them separate and incompatible. In the sense of freedom from delusion, disillusionment may be said to be a state of mind roughly approximating the disintoxication which Santayana sees as the fundamental requisite of the spiritual life and the primary attribute of the spiritual mind. Understood in this way, disillusionment does not embitter and lead toward cynicism; on the contrary, it leads toward self-knowledge and self-transcendence.

The relationship between irony, disillusionment, and the spiritual point of view may be stated in this way. Disillusionment, understood not as a painfully negative psychological state but as a state of disintoxication, is the product of the ironic double-vision which is in turn the gift of the spiritual point of view. As has several times been noted, Cabell conceives of the creative writer in the moment of creation as approaching something very much like Santayana's viewpoint of spirit. We may go further and say that the creative writer insofar as he follows the natural bent of spirit and looks only to the world of ideal essences (illusions) is a romanticist.[21] Insofar as he consents to look down from his lofty height of spirituality upon actual existence, he is the comic writer. Now the comic writer, like any other writer, insofar as he is successful, creates a work of art which makes it possible for the reader to experience the writer's point of view and, consequently, to share his attitudes. Having granted this, it is then possible to deduce what Cabell's concept of the function of comedy is: To make accessible to the reader something very like Santayana's spiritual point of view and its attitudes.

Once we have clarified the nature of irony and of disillusionment as these terms are applicable to Cabellian comedy and have grasped the function of Cabellian comedy, we can easily resolve the paradoxes upon which we stumbled earlier. It becomes clear why comedy which ultimately is said to support Aesred should initially raise a revolt against her, should play so lightly with her taboos. For if one submits at the outset and without question to the rule of Aesred, then he is debarred from the spiritual point of view and, consequently, becomes the prey of hundreds of smug, complacent little delusions which end by desiccating the soul. Absorbed in routine, wearing the blinders of custom and living wholly according to what is expected, one suffers the thwarting and repression of both his spiritual and his animal nature and vaguely feels himself to be the butt of some cruel practical joke, the point of which he does not quite see. "There is laughter overhead, but it is very far away." Life is experienced, then, as pain and frustration or as the dead weight of ennui. Therefore, some initial revolt against Aesred is necessary if man is to achieve that total and detached vision of himself and of the universe which alone can be the basis of a more or less painless, if not joyful, acceptance.

For Cabell comedy is apparently both the means of vicarious revolt and the means of ultimate acceptance. On the one hand, Cabellian comedy plays with taboos, both violating and evading them, and the comic protagonist himself is a rebel who carries the reader with him beyond the limits of the acceptable and often, especially in the later comedies, into the realm beyond common sense. On the other hand, ironically enough, this revolt in the end actually serves Aesred's purposes, a fact which, if the evidence of *Jurgen* is to be trusted, she knows full well. The flight of the comic protagonist into the wonderful, which is actually a search for the real object to which his ideal refers, teaches him that ideals are illusions and that any seeming embodiment of them merely masks the probable reality from which he has fled. Continued flight, then, is fruitless. Moreover, the comic protagonist, in comedy after comedy, discovers that there is, whether he likes it or not, a large part of his own nature to which the ministrations of Aesred are priceless.

As for the reader—sharing with the author the spiritual point of view, he sees the whole action in the light of irony with its bipartient vision of reality which holds the ideal and the actual in a comic juxtaposition. He is, so to speak, raised to the gallery of the gods; sharing their detachment, he joins in their laughter over the comic delusions of men. At the same time, insofar as the reader feels any identity of interest with the comic protagonist—insofar as he views with sympathy as well as with irony—he is placed in the position of the man who, though he has been the butt of a practical joke, sees the point and joins in the laughter of the perpetrators. In the case of Cabellian comedy, the joke is a cosmic and inexorably repeated joke; but just as the victim of the practical joke, laughing at himself, may be said to be harmonized and reconciled with his condition and with his fellows, so man, the victim of the cosmic joke, when he laughs at his own predicament may be said to be reconciled and harmonized with his own nature and with the structure of the universe.

For both the comic protagonist and the reader the result may be said to be disillusionment. (This refers merely to the reader's state of mind during the time that he surrenders to the comedy; there is no intention, of course, of attributing to the comedy any permanent or fundamental change in the psychology of the reader. It seems more likely that some degree of disillusionment in the conventional sense may be requisite to a full appreciation of Cabellian comedy.) In this state of mind it becomes possible to acknowledge the power and to submit to the reign of Aesred without the sense of unwonted compromise and frustration. For, being free from delusion, one perceives the ultimate futility of rebellion and of all action; one understands that man perforce lives in two eternally disjunct realms of being. Moreover, in his detachment the reader is able to accept the duality of his own nature, recognizing that while the human spirit finds its fulfillment in the contemplation of the ideal, it is all the same dependent upon an animal life whose objectives are quite different and that the compromises of Aesred are the best bargain man can make. Coming to terms with Aesred is also rendered easier because the recognition of the limitations and radical imperfection of all existing things leads, to borrow the words of Milton K. Munitz, "to a willingness to conform to whatever social conditions happen to prevail, since some allegiance, even when it is a matter of mere custom or habit, is necessary for one who would be a member of a given social group."[22] At the same time, the reader as well as the comic protagonist perceives that dreams and ideals are to be valued in themselves and that they can be preserved in their purity only in the realm of the imagination.[23] There they are always accessible to the imagination over which Aesred cannot of her own will extend her control; there even a featherless, wingless biped can soar with a good grace. From the elevated vantage point of spirit, the possibility of enjoying the best of both worlds, which appears to be opened up, is reassuring; the probability that man will continue to make a jumble of the two is a promise of unending comedy.

Clearly the concept of the perspective and function of comedy that has thus far been outlined does not fit (we can now say with greater weight and conviction than before) with the corrective theories of comedy. Comedy defined according to this concept may, to be sure, claim to add something to congeniality and decorum. This, however, is merely coincidental; such comedy is not primarily concerned with "man's shapeliness in the present" but rather with his attitude toward his predicament in the universe. Nor does it aim to promote the advance toward a more "logical" (that is, humanly desirable) order. For though Cabell's insistence that the proper concern of literature is with "things as they ought to be" and that the proper function of the author is to object to the inadequacy of things as they are, strongly recalls Feibleman, yet nowhere—either in his comedies or in his expository writings—does Cabell suggest that what ought to be can exist outside of the realm of the imagination or of art. Moreover, though Cabell would presumably agree with Feibleman's description of the basic comic situation as involving an unmasking of the deficiencies and limitations of the actual—the basic comic situation in Cabellian comedy might be defined more specifically as a penetration of appearances, revealing wholly elemental and probable things masquerading as ideal or wonderful things—Cabell's conception of the basic pattern of the comedy of human life, as we shall see later, explicitly rules out the possibility of allying comedy with the forces of progress. And again, Cabell would also presumably agree that at least one of the functions of comedy is "to lay bare the fictions . . . of everyday life," not, however, "with a view to founding that life more firmly"[24] but rather with the view to understanding the role of fictions and perceiving the inherently comic nature of existence. At most, Cabell's exposure of the fictions of daily life is in the interest of a wider field of fictions.

The fundamental reason for this divergence is that the perspective of Cabellian comedy is not, as Feibleman assumes the perspective of comedy must be, basically that of the ideal. It is, in fact, naturalistic. Theoretically the spiritual point of view is defined by detachment or disintoxication which makes possible a more or less objective and total view of the probable structure of the universe and of the human condition. The structure revealed might fit any of a number of possibilities, but it is clear from our earlier discussion of Cabell's world-view that for him as for Santayana the naturalistic interpretation is the most acceptable one. Now, the naturalistic interpretation leads to an acceptance of the structure of things as more or less irremediable. It results in the breaking up of the world as man experiences it into irreconcilable realms of myth and of material force; and it posits no future, heavenly or earthly, in which the ideal may be realized except possibly in part and by accident beyond human control. The naturalistic perspective makes it possible to discover the defectiveness and inadequacy of existing things by presenting them in relationship to something more desirable, closer to the ideal; but it obviously leaves little room for the idea of progress, unless one is willing to define progress purely in terms of the growth of social justice and of ephemeral social institutions. So far as Cabell is concerned, however, such progress is more apparent than real. For Cabell human life remains pretty much the same under all conditions. It may be more or less rich in imagination and emotion, but its basic pattern does not vary in essentials.

It is perhaps worth digressing briefly at this point by way of anticipating and disposing of a possible misunderstanding. If one examines Cabellian comedy in the light of Feibleman's theory, he is almost certain to be tempted to classify it as romantic comedy. According to Feibleman, "The romantic consists in a partial identification of interests with lost or perishable unique actuals. Since these must soon belong to the past, romanticism implies that perfection lies or should lie in the past rather than in the future. . . . Romantic comedy points out that though passing actuals should have been better than they were, they were better than what has taken their place. . . ."[25] Both Cabell's repeated praise of the romantic and the importance of the magical region of Antan (yesteryear) in the Biography may seem to justify such a classification. However, Cabell is very careful to make his reader aware that the tendency of man to identify the ideal with an indefinite segment of the past is the result of man's myth-making imagination which deals ruthlessly with past actualities, reshaping them in conformity with man's ideals and dreams. In other words, the glow of ideality which surrounds persons and events of the past is the outright gift of the imagination and never was theirs in fact. This Cabell makes clear in the first two books of the Biography—*Figures of Earth* and *The Silver Stallion*. These two books taken together gradually build up the ironic discrepancies not only between Don Manuel's life as he intended it and as he actually lived it but also between Don Manuel's career as his associates witnessed it and as the adherents to the cult of Manuel came to interpret it. Similarly, *The High Place* and "The Wedding Jest" cast an ironic light back over the romantic *Domnei*, revealing an impassable gulf between actuality and legend. The quest of the artist who undertakes to liberate Antan from the tyranny of Master Philologos is a somewhat different matter, but the important thing here is that this is not a quest for the recovery of an actual segment of the historical past but rather for the liberation and revitalization of the myths and legends, the ideals and dreams of mankind. Antan, like the wholly fabulous Poictesme to which Felix Kennaston manages "to return," is purely a realm of the imagination, out of time and out of space.

If Cabell's idea of comedy is to be classified under either of the two traditional headings, it clearly belongs with the cathartic theories, providing catharsis is understood as Willard Smith uses the term—the purging away of selfishness, "effecting an elevation of man's consciousness from the personal to the impersonal plane."[26] For Cabell, however, this is not simply a rising from the personal into the social plane; it is rather an emergence from the personal into what we have called the spiritual plane. The reader of Cabellian comedy is not merely watching *a* man become "the dupe of his own non-conformity" but is watching *man* become the dupe of his delusions, playing amusingly enough his role of comedian and fool of the universe.[27] Moreover, the reader comes not so much to understand the rational structure of society (though this may be an incidental by-product) as to understand the complexity of his own nature, its contradictory needs and conflicting elements, and to see with clarity and detachment the possibilities which life affords for the satisfaction of these desires as well as the limits that are set to their fulfillment. Though he sees that for the romantic idealist life must always be unsatisfactory and must end in failure, he in his moment of self-transcendence understands that: "The mishaps, the expediencies, the merry solutions of comedy, in which everybody acknowledges himself beaten and deceived, yet is somehow happier for the unexpected posture of affairs, belongs to the very texture of temporal being. . . . And if people repine at these mishaps, and rebel against these solutions, it is only because their souls are less plastic and volatile than the general flux. . . . "[28] Thus, for the moment the reader triumphs over all that from an exclusive, selfish point of view would be painful. He is prepared to be amused by life, accepting his total complex nature but not expecting actuality to assume any form that will be wholly satisfying.

Comedy which seeks to provide for such moments of self-transcendence obviously exceeds the limits laid down by Willard Smith as well as by Lane Cooper in the development of their cathartic theories of comedy. It aims not so much at the harmonization of man with his fellows as at the harmonization of man with the universe and of the conflicting elements within man's own nature, and thereby it trespasses upon the purlieus of tragedy and approaches an identity with it.

This breakdown of the usual distinction between the function of comedy and the function of tragedy does not, of course, imply the absence of all distinction. It is significant that Cabell is not given to discussing the function of literature under the categorical headings of comedy and tragedy. All literature has for him a common function; yet at the same time he does implicity recognize at least an emotional difference when he states that man, the inveterate comedian, does now and again touch the hem of tragedy's gown.[29] This suggests metaphorically both the rapprochement of the tragic and the comic and the notion that the tragic sense arises partially out of a close identification of interests with the individual comedian. This in turn suggests that, while comedy and tragedy may share a common function in that they both bring about self-transcendence with its attendant harmonization and repose, their means are in no way similar. For while comedy, as Cabell apparently understands it, provides for self-transcendence through disintoxication, a more detached and broader vision of reality, tragedy provides for self-transcendence through the intense identification of our interests with those of someone in some way greater than ourselves who lives and suffers greatly, and by rendering the suffering of this person significant. However, the life of man, built as it is in the Cabellian view upon the substanceless stuff of dreams, affords only "a thin sustenance for the tragic muse," for man fallen from the height of his illusions or overwhelmed by accident or by physiological decay is not man fallen from real eminence before fate or the blows of the gods. According to Cabell, the death of the individual is the one possible occasion for a tragic response to life, but seen in relation to the life force of which the individual is only a momentary embodiment, death itself is unreal.[30] Whatever may be the fate of its individual embodiments, the life force, though redundant, is resilient and endlessly fruitful and successful in the evasion of the snares and obstacles which beset it. By implication the tragic vision is, then, the more restricted and the less true. In Cabell's view the traditional ranking of comedy and tragedy is inverted; however compelling the illusion of tragedy, it is in comedy that we "see life steady and see it whole."

Among the commentators presented at the beginning of this chapter, only Feibleman and Cook recognize and define a form of comedy which lies outside the scope of normal comedy and which in some ways encroaches upon tragedy. For Feibleman this is divine comedy; for Cook it is serene comedy. Though ultimately Cabell's concept of comedy is distinct from the theories of both Feibleman and Cook, yet it has numerous points of contact with them and it is fruitful to explore these points of contact as a means of further clarifying Cabell's idea.

According to Feibleman, "Divine comedy criticizes almost with love, and at a very high level. Forgotten or rendered unimportant are its personal and contemporary references, and with them its bitterness has largely departed. . . . It has judgment without criticism, laughter but above the battle; and an affirmation which is almost direct. It takes all actuality as its province and contrasts it with the whole of the logical order. What remains is closer to tragedy" than to normal comedy. It is closer to tragedy because it is "directed at nothing less than the whole field of the finite predicament" and because it discovers that at least here and there "the malice of actual events may be symbolically logical"; that is, it discovers that the ideal, logical order is working itself out through, or is expressed in, actual events, and thereby it fosters "the uncritical acceptance" of things as they are.[31]

The similarities between Cabell's concept of comedy and Feibleman's concept of divine comedy are not at all recondite. Cabellian comedy does aim at "nothing less than the whole field of the finite predicament" and the laughter which it evokes is indeed "above the battle," providing this is not understood to exclude rigorously all incidental satire aimed at contemporary targets. Significantly, John Charteris in *Beyond Life* argues that the contemporary is accessible to art only insofar as it can be made to express symbolically the fundamental and timeless experiences of humanity.[32] However, Feibleman's definition of divine, as of normal, comedy is finally too narrow to accommodate Cabellian comedy. Feibleman, thoroughly committed to the theory of comedy as "an adjunct of the revolutionary principle," cannot admit or does not see the possibility of a comic perspective which does not either promote progress or nullify the need for progress in the vision of a better world to come. Feibleman's example of divine comedy is the obvious and convenient one, Dante's *Divine Comedy;* and Dante, a Christian viewing the finite predicament from the assumed vantage point of an ideally ordered next world, does achieve an "affirmation which is almost direct" because he perceives that the inequities and defects of actual earthly life are remedied in that ideally ordered next world and that, in a sense, they foreshadow and prepare for that next world.

The basically naturalistic perspective of Cabellian comedy, however, clearly provides no such basis for affirmation. The essential pattern of Cabellian comedy—a pattern which is, of course, determined by the perspective—is unvarying, and man, the eternal comedian, is bound to it, as to the wheel of Karma, without hope of release. For, as Cabell perceives it, the comedy of man is cyclical and redundant, being repeated with greater or lesser clarity in the life of every individual of every generation: "I do not find the comedy ever to be much altered in its essentials. . . . I incline to accept, in brief, that same summary of each human life which Horvendile delivered to Florian de Puysange beside the asherah stone. The first act is the imagining of a place where contentment exists and may be come to; and the second act reveals the striving toward; and the third act the falling short of, that shining goal, or else (the difference here being negligible) the attaining of it— to discover that happiness, after all, abides a thought further down the bogged, rocky, clogged, befogged heart-breaking road, if anywhere. That is the comedy which, to my finding, the life of Manuel has enacted over and yet over again upon every stage between Poictesme and Lichfield."[33] Not only does this envision succession without progress but it fails completely to envision anything beyond the final act of any individual production of this endlessly revived comedy of human life.

Yet despite the tone of pathos and futility which invests Cabell's own description of the unfleshed skeleton of his comedies, it is true that Cabellian comedy in general does achieve an "affirmation which is almost direct," an acquiescence which is not the acquiescence of despair. A matter which Feibleman treats as a subordinate point in his discussion of divine comedy is highly pertinent here: according ot Feibleman, divine comedy, unlike other comedy, may enter into the personal perspective of the protagonist as well as into the social perspective, and in so doing discovers that public failure is often private success or, at least, that the protagonist "does not lose, cannot lose, in a game in which there is no such thing as winning."[34] This entering into more than one perspective with its consequent discovery or realization, which comes to the reader if not to the protagonist, is the basis of the happy resolution in Cabellian comedy. For the reader of Cabellian comedy, finding refuge in the "plane of spirituality" rather than in Feibleman's ideal logical order, views the action from several different viewpoints simultaneously—from the viewpoint of spirit, which is overall and detached; from the viewpoint of the self-conscious but imperfectly self-realized protagonist; and from the viewpoint of the protagonist's total, complex, and contradictory nature.

Consequently, while the reader realizes that from one point of view "the malice of events" stamps the conclusion of every man's life not only with *fini* but with failure, he also discovers that the malice of events is not symbolically logical—it is ironically benevolent.

This complexity of viewpoint is not, of course, at all suggested by Cabell's summary description of his comedies, and, in fact, this summary description is a gross oversimplification, for it considers the action of the comedies from one point of view only, that of the comic protagonist in his role as romantic searcher. It is only when one considers the fully developed comedies that the complexity of viewpoint becomes apparent, and then one discovers that the pattern of vision, striving, and failure is presented in such a way as to be susceptible to more than one interpretation and that another pattern is combined with or super-imposed upon what Cabell describes as the basic pattern. This second pattern is in many ways reminiscent of the pattern which Albert Cook finds in serene comedy.

According to Cook "In serene comedy of wonderful-as-probable (or vice versa), the pattern becomes: expulsion of the searcher (the culmination of the tragic play like *Lear, Hamlet,* or *Richard II*), his experiences in the wonderful, his self-rehabilitation with new knowledge into control of society."[35] With some modification this formula can be accommodated fairly well to Cabellian comedy. First of all, it would not be accurate to speak of Cabell's comic protagonists as expelled from normal society. It is because they are searchers, longing for the wonderful and chafing under the restraints and dissatisfactions of the actual, that they seize of their own volition some opportunity to escape into the wonderful. Secondly (this is perhaps not so much a modification as an elaboration), their experiences in the wonderful lead them to discover the probable-in-the-wonderful. And, thirdly, they do not return into control of society because their rehabilitation is by way of compromise and because the magical powers which assist them in the realm of the wonderful are not transferable to the realm of the actual. Still, despite these qualifications, the journey into the wonderful followed by a return to and reconciliation with the probable norms of society does define the movement of Cabellian comedy.

It is probably no accident, then, that the same two works—the *Odyssey* and *The Tempest*—which Cook uses as the basis for his definition of serene comedy receive prominent mention in Cabell's works. Indeed, one of the major motifs of *Jurgen*—what we might call the homing motif—is borrowed from the *Odyssey*, and the novel may be read as a blending of the Odyssean and the Faustian legends. It would, of course, be impossible to say to what extent Cabell's idea of comedy was shaped by his interest in these two works, but it is safe to say that Cabellian comedy in its fully matured form is of their type if not of their class. It shares with them a similar movement and a similar function, although the means by which that function is fulfilled differ.

Cook is not as clear as he might be about the function of what he defines as serene comedy. Presumably, however, its function must be in line with, at least compatible with, his general theory of comedy as ritual expulsion, which assumes that comedy witnesses to the sanctity of the norms of society by providing an occasion for the expulsion, by means of laughter, of the abnormal pariah. According to this theory, comedy is essentially conservative; it identifies health with the social norms and rejoices over the preservation and triumph of these norms. Following this line of thought, it is possible to assign a similar function to serene comedy. The wonderful, which in Cook's theory plays a large part in serene comedy, normally lies within the province of tragedy,[36] and the very existence of that which may be classified as wonderful—for example, death, mystery, romantic love, transcendent moral law—challenges the norms of society. Moreover, the searcher of serene comedy is the would-be pariah. Normal comedy denies the first and expels the second, but serene comedy subsumes them both and renders them innocuous by purging them of their tragic implications. It accomplishes this either by showing that practical wisdom and diplomacy can prevail against the wonderful (the *Odyssey*) or by representing the experience of the wonderful as the basis of practical social wisdom and as ultimately leading to the rehabilitation of the pariah to the social norms *(The Tempest)*. Serene comedy, though its vision is more inclusive, is also conservative in function, serving to affirm the social norms and to put men at ease in the presence of the wonderful.

As we have seen, the function of Cabellian comedy may be described in somewhat similar terms; it, too, is ultimately conservative and aims to put men at ease in the presence of mystery. It might even be argued that Cabellian comedy in part fulfills its function by subordinating the wonderful to the probable which is the basis of the social norms, for everywhere the active pursuit of the wonderful is shown to end in wholly probable experience, and in the end the wonderful illusions of the poet and the idealist make room for the illusions of stability and security, to be gained through compliance with the social norms. This, however, is not quite what we have in the *Odyssey* or in *The Tempest*. Again it is perspective and focus which make the difference.

In both the *Odyssey* and *The Tempest* the realm of the wonderful is accepted as having independent existential status; it can, therefore, be brought into some sort of harmony with the probable world of social experience and can be made to yield powers and wisdom which are applicable for the good of society. Moreover, though serene comedy allows for far greater concern with the individual than does ordinary comedy, its focus—insofar as this is defined by the *Odyssey* and *The Tempest*—is nonetheless social. For both Prospero and Odysseus are rulers, that is, socially significant people. What they do or fail to do has serious social implications which the reader is never allowed to forget. Prospero, the pariah-magician, could use his abnormal powers destructively, but his equally abnormal wisdom constrains him to use them only in the interest of the health of the social norms—honest administration, love and marriage. The return of Odysseus to Ithaca means the preservation of the integrity of the ruling family; therefore, his triumph over the wonderful forces which oppose him not only is an endorsement of the social values of diplomacy and expediency, which he in some degree represents, but is directly related to the continuity and stability of society.

By contrast, Cabellian comedy with its basically naturalistic perspective does not accept the wonderful in the simple, unquestioning manner of the *Odyssey* and *The Tempest;* it holds the wonderful experiences of the comic protagonist in the dual focus of irony. The consequences of this are several. First of all it means that the reader is aware at all times that the realm of the wonderful is man's own creation, called forth by man's dissatisfaction with things as they are, and that, while the actual (probable) can cloak itself in the appearances of the wonderful, the two realms can never be fused or harmonized. This in turn means that such harmonization as is achieved must take place within the individual; it must be the harmonization of man's "double-soul."[37] These consequences of the difference in perspective are closely related to a difference in focus. Paradoxically, though in Cabellian comedy the reader feels less closely identified with the protagonist than he does with, say, Prospero and Odysseus, yet the focus is individual rather than social. The relatively greater detachment in Cabellian comedy is due to the fact that the comic protagonists, unlike Prospero and Odysseus, are representative human beings; they embody typical attitudes and experience a fate which is typical, however individual in appearance and in particulars. Given Cabell's worldview and his general comic vision, it could hardly be otherwise. Moreover, the ironic light in which the actions and experiences of the comic protagonists are presented re-enforces the detachment which one generally feels in the presence of the typical.

At the same time, the Cabellian comic protagonist, unlike Prospero and Odysseus, is not, at least initially, a significant social figure. He acts in a personal rather than a social context. His self-willed journey into the wonderful is undertaken for personal reasons; he returns to society for personal reasons. At no time are the social implications of his actions stressed; neither by being outside of society nor by returning to it does he seriously affect the social norms. Of course, if we consider the Cabellian comic protagonist as the symbol of the human spirit in its total and eternal manifestation, the comedy takes on implications which transcend both the individual and the social; for then his revolt against the probable norms of human experience and his quest for the wonderful threaten the whole structure of conventions and fictions upon which the human spirit really depends for its survival.[38] This consideration, however, is a part of the general background of the total *Biography of Manuel* and does not enter into the immediate response to the individual comedies, though it is no doubt a necessary condition of that ultimate repose and acquiescence at which Cabellian comedy in general aims.

An important result of the lack of social emphasis is that the feeling of success which is essential to Cabellian comedy, as to all comedy, cannot be so easily rendered in social terms as it can be even in what Cook defines as serene comedy. Society *qua* society may, of course, take some satisfaction in the return of the searcher; his return means one more conformist, one less bad example. Moreover, from the practical pragmatic viewpoint of society the journey of the searcher into the wonderful ends in predestined failure, and this may be taken as an indirect affirmation of the wisdom and health of the social norms. But while these negative occasions for the rejoicing of society are present, they are decidedly not stressed.

In order to understand the terms of success in Cabellian comedy, we must recall once again that Cabell's comic protagonist is a complex, a divided and contradictory, and, unlike Prospero and Odysseus, a highly protean being. Moreover, though from an absolute point of view as well as from the practical social point of view he fails, the reader has known all along that the protagonist played at a game in which "there is no such thing as winning" and in which, consequently, all success must be counted relative.

Given these conditions, the protagonist, though he cannot succeed in the sense of attaining all that he desires, can fail in at least two possible ways. He can fail by losing the sustaining sense of his own dignity and importance or by the hypertrophy of one aspect of his nature at the expense of the other aspects, resulting either in the cutting away of his roots in nature, which means madness and premature destruction, or in a loss of contact with the realm of the ideal through the withering away of the imagination. Success negatively considered means avoiding these possibilities; positively, it is the retention of his invaluable sense of dignity coupled with the healthy satisfaction, within the unavoidable limits, of both animal and spiritual needs. In these terms, the Cabellian comic protagonist aided by his vanity, his dullness, and his divided and mutable nature, is successful. As we have already seen— even though the protagonist's animal nature finds gratification where his spiritual nature had thought to find it, yet for the satisfaction of his spiritual nature there has been the vision of the ideal and "the certain hour" in which for a moment the ideal seemed to be realized. And though the course of his wanderings in the wonderful may bring him, as it does Jurgen and Florian de Puysange and Gerald Musgrave, to the brink of spiritual bankruptcy, the relative repleteness of vision and of appetite and the natural abating of animal and spiritual vigor (the malice of time) breed a qualified contentment, a mood of compromise and acceptance.

That this concluding mood is the result of a somewhat precarious equilibrium, two of Cabell's fables, "Prologue of Duke Prospero at Milan" and "Epilogue of True Thomas by Moonlight," testify;[39] yet, it is the thriftiest bargain man can come by, and in the context it is as satisfying as Prospero's "We are such stuff/As dreams are built on, and our little life/Is rounded with a sleep," which, coming at the end of The Tempest's strange blend of political intrigue, supernatural powers, and idyllic love, seems to put at rest all of the anxieties and tensions of human existence and to dispose quietly of the problems of good and evil and of destiny.

Cabellian comedy differs, then, from comedy as generally defined in scope, in perspective, and in function. Like all comedy, Cabellian comedy might be defined as an overtly artificial experience designed to arouse comic laughter through the contemplation of the disproportionate, the incongruous, the ridiculous; but Cabell does not limit his subject matter to man in society or to man as a social being. His subject matter is individual man pursuing his own isolated though typical destiny. Moreover, while Cabell thinks in terms of typical categories and attitudes, the perspective of his comedy is not that of society or of the group. Nor does he accept the ideal logical order as providing the only proper perspective for comedy. Though his method is in part to reveal the inadequacies of actuality in relation to what is ideal or desirable, his perspective remains at bottom naturalistic—a situation which leads to the simultaneous endorsement of the ideal, on the one hand, and the acceptance of the actual as inevitable and irremediable, on the other. Generally speaking, his comedy aims at "the whole of the finite predicament"; its source is the essential pattern of human living seen against the background of a naturalistically conceived cosmos.

The function of Cabellian comedy is implicit in its perspective and scope. If it is to be associated with either of the traditional theories of function, it must be with the cathartic theories, for Cabellian comedy clearly aims to lift the reader from the plane of egoistic self-absorption to the plane of spirituality, thus making available to him the comic vision of reality. It lifts him temporarily out of the stream of life, the flux of things; it relieves him for the time being of the necessity of participation; and seating him, so to speak, in the gallery of the gods, it allows him to witness more or less objectively the humorous antics of man pursuing in his clumsy and comic and at times pathetic way his particular delusions and presuming upon the thin stuff of his rationality for support. Through the irony and total understanding which are the concomitants of the vision, the reader's sense of proportion is corrected; he perceives clearly the inadequacies and defectiveness of actual existence, but joining in the laughter of the gods, he triumphs over the finite predicament, over all that for the feeling subject and from an exclusive, selfish point of view would be painful.

Thus, in its function Cabellian comedy approaches tragedy, for like tragedy it seeks to adjust man to the conditions of the universe and to harmonize the conflicting elements within man's own nature. Whereas, however, tragedy achieves its purpose through an intense personal identification of interests with those of the protagonist and through the sense that out of waste and suffering some value emerges that would not otherwise exist, Cabellian comedy, like all comedy, achieves its ends through detachment and through the sense that such limited success as is possible to man is purchased not at the price of a waste of spirit but of quite ordinary qualities of mind—a kind of hand-to-mouth shrewdness and adaptability coupled with ultimate obtuseness and vanity and an inherent propensity to dream. Tragedy triumphs over the finite predicament by accepting all that is painful in that predicament as the necessary condition for the emergence of the godlike in man; Cabellian comedy triumphs over the finite predicament by giving at least the impression of understanding the exact terms of that predicament and by suggesting that in the very malice of time and events and death there may lie hidden an unsought and ironic benevolence. Moreover, whereas tragic irony stresses the awesome possibilities of existence, the irony in Cabellian comedy reveals all experience outside of the realm of the imagination to be platitudinous: everywhere and always action leads to purely probable experience. However disappointing this may be to the romantic and the poet who make a part of every man, it is laughable to the disintoxicated mind and comforting to the everyday citizen.

The end at which Cabellian comedy finally aims is the clear yet serene awareness of the conditions of human existence. It is the quiet disillusionment of Prospero's "We are such stuff as dreams are built on" or, perhaps more precisely, of Santayana's "I am quite happy in this human ignorance mitigated by pictures, for it yields practical security and poetic beauty: what more can a sane man want?"

5

The Early Comedies

Meredith's dictum that comedy has nothing to do with man's essential nature or with his destiny is no doubt too restrictive; yet most commentators and theorists agree that comedy is at any rate a pre-eminently mundane affair, that it treats of ordinary men (perhaps depressed below the norm) in the more or less commonplace circumstances of everyday life. Observation, of course, bears out this contention. Aristophanes may deal playfully with the Greek gods and upon occasion may repair to Hades or to Cloudcuckootown and Molière may imply through a Tartuffe or through an Alcestis a great deal about man's nature, but with rare exception the focus of the comedy remains social, its subject matter the behavior of man in society.

That this should be so is not difficult to understand. Only the bigot or the chauvinist could hold the social behavior of man in any given time to be wholly rational, consistent, or heroic, and therefore the generality of men are capable of viewing the problems and experiences of everyday social life from a comic viewpoint. However, the farther the comic writer diverges from this comic norm, the more difficult it is for him to sustain the comic attitude and to elicit a comic response. For the farther he pene-

63

trates into man's fundamental nature and into the human predicament, the greater the number of affective values that are disturbed and that the comic spirit must somehow lay to rest if the comic attitude is not to be destroyed.

If, then, the subject of the comedy is, as it is ultimately for Cabell, the structure of the universe and of the human psyche, the writer's problem is a complex one. The difficulty of making a small segment of man's social experience reflect a broad comic philosophy of the nature of things is clear enough; social comedy turned to such purposes usually must make room for "philosophical" discourse or a "philosophical" commentator, neither of which is particularly compatible with that mood of playfulness which comedy requires. At best they can be assimilated to the comic mood by means of verbal wit and paradox, whimsey and flippancy. The chapter entitled "Kennaston Speaks the Parabasis" in *The Eagle's Shadow* is an example of this method. Of course *Beyond Life* is something of a *tour de force* in the same vein. Then again, if the comic writer chooses to be more inclusive in his treatment of contemporary life, he is handicapped both by the restricting demands of verisimilitude and by the ever-present risk of stirring up a hornets' nest of special interests and preoccupations in which are invested those strong emotions most hostile to the comic spirit. The first of these handicaps is particularly hampering to a writer, like Cabell, to whom neither the universe at large nor the real experience of any man conforms to the conventional notions of verisimilitude, and to whom the important thing is to express not so much the comic irony of any given human life at any given moment but the comic irony of all human living. The second of these handicaps, of course, involves the problem of distance or detachment. Detachment is the *sine qua non* of the comic mood. If the reader's ego is bruised or if he is made to feel that the emotions and attitudes which he believes to be deep and serious have been betrayed, his capacity for comedy is instantly diminished. So-called sentimental comedy is the obvious solution here and, therefore, the obvious pitfall, for sentimental comedy pays obeisance to the familiar emotions, stirs them gently and superficially in passing, mixes tears with langhter, and comes to rest finally in the warm glow of a conventional happy ending. Such a facile solution is a very inadequate vehicle for attitudes which are as complex as are those of Cabell.

Cabell did not find an immediate answer to all or any of these problems, though it may well be—evidence is necessarily lacking here—that the problems themselves only gradually emerged as his point of view matured and that his technical ability merely kept pace with the increasingly severe demands of his art. At any rate, ultimately, after exploring the possibilities of the comedy of manners and of romantic comedy, he discovered an adequate technique which is more or less uniquely his own. What Cabell came in time to write are fantasies or, more accurately, comic allegories compounded of myth and folklore refurbished for new allegorical and symbolic purposes. As Cabell himself explained it, he created Poictesme—the sometimes mythical, sometimes pseudohistorical realm in which his fantasies take place—because he needed in his art to be omnipotent; he needed a world unencumbered by any laws other than those of his own making.[1] As the completed *Biography of Manuel* now stands, it is the story of man's relations, both personal and indirect, with that mythical realm.

What Cabell gained by means of his technique of comic allegory and fantasy is manifold. By carrying the reader to a land beyond common sense, Cabell achieves that atmosphere of holiday detachment which John Charteris in *Beyond Life* recommends, without having to resort to the rather stale and sterile setting of the drawing room or somebody's house party. By plunging the reader into a milieu which superficially has little or nothing to do with the familiar world, Cabell succeeds in putting to rest all the numerous predispositions and affections which ordinarily determine the way in which man views his own most serious doings as well as those of his fellows. More important than this, however, by borrowing widely from myth, legend, and folklore, Cabell is able to give concrete, dramatic expression to his otherwise abstract concepts. Out of the fragments of many mythologies and folklores, augmented by his own invention, Cabell created a pantheon of deities who, besides being susceptible to comic treatment, bring with them a nimbus of far-reaching associations. Their presence gives, without discourse, an immediate depth of meaning. Moreover, they combine in themselves two aspects which are fundamental to the expression of Cabell's world-view; they simultaneously represent the dead dreams by means of which man has in the past explained his world and himself, and the living forces that continue to shape man's life both from within and from without. Somewhat similarly the pseudolegendary figures whom Cabell uses as his comic protagonists extend the meaning without sacrificing either action or comedy. For without losing their own individuality they subsume the characters of other significant legendary figures. Thus, Jurgen is not Faust nor Odysseus nor the Wandering Jew but partakes of all of them and yet remains Jurgen. The consequence is that Jurgen's deeds and experiences are broadly representative, or at least suggestive, of general human experience in a way in which, say, Colonel Musgrave's or George Bulmer's can never be.

The service of these useful allegorical and symbolic figures is not the only advantage that Cabell drew from his interest in myth and folklore. Equally important is the fact that in the conventions of myths and folk tales he has found the basis for the laws of Poictesme. These conventions are particularly well suited to the expression of Cabell's vision of man as journeying through an irrational universe in which he blunders from mystery to mystery feeling himself assaulted and moved by strange forces but sustained by faith in his own sanity and cleverness; a universe in which nothing is what it appears and in which ends are predictable but seldom implicit in beginnings. Moreover, while the conventions of myths and folk tales do not conform to what science describes as the natural laws of the universe, they do express fundamental dreams and experiences of the human psyche, and these dreams and experiences are, of course, for Cabell the really important stuff of every human life and, thus, of the comedy of human existence. It may be, too, that the general association of fantasy and fairy tales with childhood helps to foster the playfulness which, initially at least, is essential to the experience of comedy.

All in all, the technique of fantasy and comic allegory which Cabell ultimately developed makes it possible for him to deal with the broad general patterns of human living without sacrificing either concreteness or the playfulness and the comic irony which are fundamental to his point of view.

Neither the concept of comedy elaborated in the preceding chapter nor the techniques discussed immediately above are apparent in Cabell's early works. Though Cabell managed by one means and another to assimilate even his earliest published materials into the finished structure of *The Biography of Manuel* (the essay entitled "The Comedies of William Congreve," which appeared originally in the *International* for April, 1901, now forms a part of *Beyond Life*), his world-view, his concept of comedy, and his ultimate techniques were apparently all gradually evolved over a period of roughly nineteen years. According to Cabell's own account, the evolution of the Biography began "as far back as 1901, when I wrote, in 'The Love-Letters of Falstaff,' the first of the stories afterward bound up together as *The Line of Love*,"[2] but even a small amount of casual browsing through the early unrevised editions of the books earlier than *The Cream of the Jest* and especially through the magazine versions of the short stories that have since been incorporated into the Biography is sufficient to reveal that the themes and attitudes which were later to dominate the complete work were present in the beginning, if at all, only in fragmentary and embryonic form. Even if one merely rearranges the individual books in the order of publication, he will quickly perceive a pattern of growth, a line of development, which the final arrangement of the Storisende edition more or less successfully conceals.

The Line of Love (1905) may, as Cabell suggests, have contained the germ of the Biography, but only insofar as it, like the longer work, is ostensibly a family chronicle, a series of episodes bound together by their mutual relationship to a single family tree, and insofar as the individual stories making up the volume explore tentatively the three fundamental attitudes later developed—the chivalrous, the gallant, and the poetic—as these attitudes are reflected in the love affairs of men and women and modified by time. Yet neither in spirit nor in scope does *The Line of Love* as it appeared in 1905 adequately foreshadow the Biography. When Cabell came to rewrite the early book for the Kalki edition in 1921, he added "The Wedding Jest" and "Porcelain Cups" in order to round out the treatment of the three attitudes and to bring the perspective and tone into line with that of the rest of the Biography. Still later Cabell felt it necessary to write, in the later comic allegorical style, *The Music from behind the Moon* (1926), *The White Robe* (1928), and *The Way of Ecben* (1929) in order to present "in epitome, the three strivings in which the descendants of Manuel are . . . involved."[3]

A chronological list of Cabell's short stories and comedies published between 1902 and 1915 does, however, reflect a fairly systematic exploration of the three basic attitudes later epitomized in *The Witch Woman* trilogy. Thus, the attitude of gallantry predominates in the period roughly from 1902 to 1907, the chivalrous attitude in the period from 1907 to 1911, and the poetic attitude in the period from 1911 to 1915. Moreover, there is present from the beginning the sense of man's general inadequacy for his self-imposed role and of the shadow that falls between the intention and the performance, the promise and the deed. There is accordingly a faint, scarcely enforced touch of irony in much of the early work, but for the most part in the early stories—for instance, those bound up in *The Line of Love* and in *Gallantry*—Cabell seems to have been chiefly concerned with gestures, romantic or gallant. He was a long way from finding the means whereby to render (if he saw it) the general significance of the gesture or to make it yield comedy without wholly giving up its impressiveness or beauty. Thus, these gestures of an Arnaye, a Villon, an Ormskirk remain personal, romantic, and in themselves trivial. Their creator has an eye for landscapes and an ear for repartee and high-flown speeches, but he lacks perspective and detachment and consequently seems to invest in his creatures far more faith and emotion than is warranted.

Moreover, the early exploration of the three basic attitudes was done in terms of representative figures, historical and pseudo-historical, which are dominated by the conventions of historical romance and by the popular stereotypes of the day. Villon is the conventional *poète maudit,* dear to the writers of the late nineteenth century decadence and to the general mood of the *fin de siècle;* Adhelmar is anyone's vision of the chivalrous knight in the days when knighthood was in flower; Ormskirk is almost wholly a creation of the popular theater. Though it is probably not completely true that the young Cabell aspired merely to write "some wholesome and nice entertaining books, that would sell like *The Cardinal's Snuff-Box* and *The Prisoner of Zenda*,"[4] yet it is true that these early stories in their unrevised form bear the distinct impress of the popular taste in magazine fiction of the day—the high color and florid rhetoric of Graustark romance, the frothy drawing room wit and paradox hunting that filled the pages of the old *Smart Set,* and the idyllic mood of the retreat to Arden.

A comparison of the 1905 edition of *The Line of Love,* which Cabell ranks as his first published book, with the 1928 Storisende edition of the same book reveals something of the gulf which separates the attitudes and the point of view of the beginning writer from those of the mature author. In all cases of revision of the books preceding *The Cream of the Jest* much of Cabell's care has, of course, gone into the interpolation of information and allusions—often nothing more than name dropping—which serve to bind the diverse volumes of the Biography into a single structure; but beyond this, Cabell's revision has been largely a matter of toning down the diction and of re-enforcing the comic irony. In rewriting *The Line of Love,* Cabell has accomplished the toning down by the simple expedient of deleting the more flagrant theatrical and romantic clichés, by numerous substitutions of less highly emotive words, and by the introduction of a note of greater frankness which constantly calls attention to the substratum of biological necessity that underlies the high-flown gestures. Thus, Adhelmar "swore in his soul that Hagues must die that this woman might be his wife" becomes "so that this woman might be Adhelmar's bedfellow"; and "Then, at last, I sickened in Amsterdam three years ago" becomes "Then, at last, I got a clap in Amsterdam, three years ago."[5]

The means by which Cabell re-enforced the comic irony are more complex. First of all, in the Storisende edition he has done this by means of additions to "The Epistle Dedicatory" and to the "Envoi" and by highlighting, in the head links, the incongruity between the moment of noble sentiment recorded in the stories and the general tenor and outcome of the lives these lovers actually lived thereafter. In the dedication and the envoi of the 1905 edition, Cabell cast himself in the role of the self-conscious apologist for the love story, pitting himself against the sturdy common sense of Mrs. Grundy and the theorizing of Schopenhauer, insisting that, from whatever point of view, love is important. All in all, the dedication and envoi merely echo the familiar formulations of the 1890's; they do not even hint at an inclination to view these love affairs, for all their nobility of gesture and fineness of phrase, as, after all, but the fragments of a general comedy of existence.

In the Storisende edition, a lengthy passage interpolated in "The Epistle Dedicatory" shifts the emphasis from the significance of love as the agent which brings us to our "finest hour" to the comic repetitiousness of all love affairs: "She [Nature] aims, it would appear, but to repeat unblushingly in every human life the same lectual comedy, to the same end. And when you reflect that since Sumeria was, there has developed no real change in the comedy, and no varying in the illusions which induce it . . . then it seems quite apparent that the condition of Nature is pathological." Another fairly lengthy interpolation in the "Envoi" serves to bring the brief love stories of the early work within the larger perspective of the Biography: "And if that hour did not ever have its sequel in precisely the life-long rapture, nor always in a wedding with the person preferred, yet since, at any rate, it resulted in a marriage that turned out well enough, in a world wherein people have to consider expediency, one may rationally assert that each of these romances ended happily. Besides, there had been the hour. . . ."

Besides these modifications made in the framework of the book (modifications which add up to a considerable alleviation of the self-conscious romanticism and callowness of the original), Cabell added, in the Kalki edition of 1921, the two stories already mentioned, "The Wedding Jest" and "Porcelain Cups," and later made considerable alterations in the point of view of several of the other stories. "The Wedding Jest" expresses allegorically what Cabell by 1921 had apparently come to see as the comic theme of the book—the deathless susceptibility of men to the trite illusions of love in the face of all possible disillusionment. As for "Porcelain Cups," Cabell found in the hero, Kit Marlowe, a convenient means of expressing explicitly the fundamental source of the comedy of human existence which is reflected briefly and inadequately in the earlier edition of *The Line of Love.* "It is not your fault [says Marlowe to a woman who has betrayed his trust] that every now and then is born a man who serves an ideal which is to him the most important thing in the world. It is not your fault that this man perforce inhabits a body to which the most important thing in the world is a woman. Certainly it is not your fault that the compost makes yet another jumble of the two desires, and persuades himself that the two are somehow allied."[6]

The changes in point of view Cabell made in some of the other stories which were originally included in the edition of 1905 serve uniformly to undercut the rampant romanticism of the chivalric pieces and to temper the pathos and romantic irony of others. Thus, in the Storisende edition the chivalrous posturing of Fulke d'Arnaye is seen through the now sophisticated eyes of Adelais who is both impatient with his "top-lofty nonsense" and flattered by it. Significantly, her inner voice is already that of the practical, commonplace wife. Thus, too, the romantic irony of "In Necessity's Mortar" is modulated by a new ending which suddenly forces upon the reader distance and detachment from the subject: "And straight way he perceived that triple invocation could be, rather neatly, worked out in ballade form. . . . Yes, with a separate prayer to each verse. So, dismissing for the while his misery, he fell to considering, with undried cheeks, the rhymes he needed."[7] Emotions so lightly turned aside are not to be taken too seriously.

When the first of Cabell's books, then, is compared with its own final version as it stands in the Storisende edition of *The Biography of Manuel,* it becomes apparent that, at the least, Cabell's earliest work lacked restraint and, more important than that, lacked the detachment and the genuine sophistication needed to perceive the larger pattern of the comedy of human living reflected even in the moments of noble sentiment and high passion which *The Line of Love* ostensibly records. As has been said, Cabell's interest was apparently almost wholly absorbed in the gesture, in rendering the appropriate posture and emotion of the moment. His penchant for humor and irony was evident but gave little promise of his future mastery. The irony found in this first work—for example, in "The Castle of Content" and in "In Necessity's Mortar"—is a somewhat sentimental romantic irony which re-enforces rather than qualifies the characters' estimation of themselves and of their situation. It emanates directly from the characters, is part of their emotional experience, and in no way enlarges or complicates the reader's perspective. As for humor—only the two pseudo-Shakespearian pieces, "The Love-Letters of Falstaff" and "In Ursula's Garden," are intentionally humorous. The first of these borrows a set of characters from the history plays, the second its atmosphere and situation from the romantic comedies; both of them owe such comic buoyancy as they have to a decidedly second-hand Shakespearian wit.

However, though these very early stories scarcely foreshadow Cabell's later development as a comic writer, the fact that the influence of Shakespeare lies like a visible shadow upon at least two of them is, in retrospect, significant. Similarly palpable outcroppings of Shakespeare's influence were to appear at scattered intervals throughout the works published between 1901 and 1917. None of these are important in themselves; none of them indicate either remarkable penetration or thorough assimilation, but they do suggest that Shakespeare, perhaps even more than François Villon and Christopher Marlowe, exerted a strong magnetic attraction upon the imagination of the young Cabell. Just what the center of this magnetic attraction was or came to be is perhaps suggested by the fact that when Cabell came to use Shakespeare as a character in *The Certain Hour*,[8] he chose to write about Shakespeare, the author of *The Tempest*. When at last Cabell had developed a manner of his own, had discovered his own means of achieving something like the scope and ultimate serene equilibrium of *The Tempest,* the ghost of Shakespeare ceased, so to speak, to haunt his books in broad daylight. In the beginning, however, Cabell could only feebly imitate Shakespeare's verbal wit, his mannerisms and his typical situations.

Cabell's first attempts at writing full-scale comedies were *The Eagle's Shadow*, first published in 1904, and *Gallantry*, published in 1907. Both are in some sense comedies of manners, though the second is a historical set piece and the first is an attempt to render contemporary manners. Both are, in Cabell's term, mundicidious—light, worldly comedies which play superficially with human foibles. Both depend upon stock characters and stock situations, but *Gallantry,* because it is constrained and shaped by the spirit of the eighteenth century as that spirit had been defined in literary convention dating back at least to *Henry Esmond* and because it pretends to be nothing very serious, is the more successfully comic. Neither, however, has thematic complexity, and though many light ironies play over their surfaces, there is no fundamental underlying irony such as the later comedies are built upon.

The Eagle's Shadow is an old bag of tricks not very adroitly played. According to Cabell, he originally aimed at "that atmosphere of holiday detachment from the ordinary duties and obligations of existence" and at picturing "people solely in a temporary and irresponsible withdrawal from the everyday business of life."[9] His objective was obviously the playfulness of light comedy. Unfortunately, the house-party setting is not in itself sufficient to insure such playfulness, especially when—and this is true of Cabell's story—there is a trite but ostensibly serious theme, in this case the corrupting influence of money, which suggests that the characters and their experiences are after all to be taken with some seriousness. Such a suggestion is inevitably fatal when, as here, the characters are the almost wholly un-refurbished stock characters out of the frothiest sort of stage comedy—the gruff but tender-hearted father, the quarrelsome but meant-for-each-other young lovers, the foppish but gifted artist, the self-seeking philanthropists who, it turns out, have hearts of gold.

Yet, despite the cast of inanimate stereotypes, despite what Carl Van Doren has called the "sillabub dialogue," and despite the melodramatic climax which provides an ending without resolving the problem posed by the theme—despite all of these deficiencies, there are in *The Eagle's Shadow* a few things that faintly foreshadow later developments. First of all, it appears that even at this early date (the book was written in 1903) Cabell was already groping toward some such concept of a romantic, extemporizing demiurge as was later embodied in Horvendile. For it is Orven Deal who sends Cock-eye Flint, that abortive Dickensian intrusion, into the garden at Selwood and thus precipitates the end of the comedy, and who is later vaguely associated with "The Author of all our comedies."[10] Besides the unexplained intrusion of Deal and his pawn, which as the comedy stands appears to be no more than the most clumsily handled sort of *deus ex machina,* the comedy contains in Kennaston's "Defense of Ignorance"[11] the scarcely perceptible seed of the doctrine of dynamic illusions later elaborated by John Charteris in *Beyond Life.* The "Defense of Ignorance," however, is pure imitation Wilde. Cabell failed to endow Kennaston with either the sophistication or the range of reference or the range of wit with which in the future he was to endow John Charteris. Moreover, the "Defense of Ignorance" has no vital relationship to the comedy as a whole; at most it serves merely the irrelevant purpose of burlesquing the strained wit, the willful cynicism, and the self-conscious immorality of the so-called late nineteenth century decadents.

Turning from *The Eagle's Shadow* to *Gallantry,* which is not designated a comedy and which was written and published piecemeal between 1902 and 1907 (first published as a book in 1907), one is struck by the considerable, though possibly only apparent, gain in technical mastery. Whereas, the earlier book seems in all respects abortive, the later, even before "the more romantic passages in the best style of 1907" had been cut,[12] achieved a limited success. *Gallantry* pretends to no serious theme and to no profound irony. The book explores an attitude as it was supposedly manifested in the eighteenth century, an attitude which by intention is resolutely superficial and of which the broad outlines at least are given by convention; consequently, the writing of it involved few problems of distance or of verisimilitude. Moreover, not only does the book seek merely to incarnate the conventionally defined spirit of an earlier period, it depends largely for its comic effect upon the borrowed literary devices of that period. All the tricks of eighteenth century melodrama and farce are exploited—the unpredictable shifts in plot and character relationships arising out of concealed motivation, the farcical mix-ups (Captain Audain suddenly finds he has become his sweetheart's grandfather[13]), and the high-flown language and sentiments that fall so readily into burlesque. Moreover, the characters themselves, though like the characters in *The Eagle's Shadow* they are all stereotypes, are drawn from a more vigorous variety of comedy, and they bring with them a certain talent for witticism and repartee. They make no demand to be taken seriously by the reader; they resolutely refuse to take themselves seriously. They ask only that the reader appreciate their wit, in which after all the comedy is largely invested.

This is to say, of course, that the comedy is in the main a somewhat frothy verbal comedy and that there is in the book little real penetration of the psychology of gallantry. In Ormskirk, however, and to a lesser extent in Gaston de Puysange the roots of gallantry are obliquely glanced at. In a moment of depression Ormskirk sees "the world as an ugly mechanical drawing, fashioned for utility, meticulously outlined everywhere with a draftman's measuring rule,"[14] and both Ormskirk and Puysange see the farce of life somewhat to their pain. At bottom they are disillusioned romantics,[15] and their flippant habit of mind and their determination to play out wittily whatever role presents itself are their means of mastering despair.

The psychology of Ormskirk and of Puysange, however callowly conceived, prefigures the far more complex psychology of Jurgen, and their point of view, purged of its smell of the theater and of its tinge of sentimentality and self-indulgence, was to gain ascendancy over all the other points of view with which the Biography is ostensibly concerned. As Cabell himself pointed out, even in those books which supposedly deal with the chivalric attitude he unconsciously "shifted the main part of his interest from a chivalrous character to the nearest male character whose attitude was distinctly not chivalrous."[16] Cabell claimed to attach no particular importance to this fact, but an explanation surely is not far to seek.

The attitude of gallantry is rooted in disillusionment, is the by-product of it, and combines a playful habit of mind with the ironic double-vision. The gallant person insists, within the limits defined by Jurgen's experience, upon being honest with himself about himself and his world. At his best he knows both the price and the value of everything; in Cabell's terms he can "admire the well-turned leg of a thief" without forgetting that he is looking at a thief;[17] and, consequently, he is always somewhat detached, watching his own actions and those of his fellow men as though he were a spectator at a play, watching from a slightly elevated position with amusement but not without sympathy. Something very like this point of view—what was described in the preceding chapter as the perspective of Cabellian comedy—and the consequent tone are characteristic of Cabell's mature comedies; it is a point of view readily adapted to the purpose of rendering the comedy of the finite predicament without either sentimentality or cynicism. *Gallantry*, however, is a long way from *Jurgen*. In the former the gallant attitude and the gallant point of view are displayed only upon a narrow, conventionalized stage, and the gallant characters, clear sighted and worldly wise though they are intended to be, very rarely look beyond their immediate surroundings and their own localized doings.

When Cabell came to revise *Gallantry* for the Storisende edition, he insisted that the book is by design "frankly mundicidious," but he was aware too that it is a book of beginnings: "Poictesme began with *Gallantry*. . . . With Ormskirk began the first sketching of that afterward omnipresent person whom Mr. Thomas Beer has described as the 'talkative lover, the broken idealist of women.' And Horvendile also began with *Gallantry*—wherein . . . he wears the name of Francis Vanringham."[18] Cabell is perhaps inaccurate about the genesis of Horvendile, for the Orven Deal of *The Eagle's Shadow* would seem to have been a still earlier creation. Yet, once we have been given the clue, it is clear that Vanringham was designed for some such role as that played by Horvendile in the later comedies, though in type he is closer to Ahasuerus of *Domnei* than he is to that subtle, whimsical, and, in some indefinable way, sinister demiurge. As for Poictesme—though it is to that realm that Ormskirk goes in search of his lost youth, it is at yet scarcely more than a name. It has no distinctive history and, what is more, no mythology. All in all, it is very far from being a "land wherein human nature kept its first dignity and strength, and wherein human passions were never in a poor way to find expression with adequate speech and action."[19]

6

The Middle Comedies

           The Cords of Vanity (1909), *The Soul of Melicent*
(1913) (in the Kalki and Storisende editions entitled *Domnei: A
Comedy of Woman-Worship*), and *The Rivet in Grandfather's Neck*
(1915) were all written within a period of five years, 1907 to 1912.
The first and last of these explore two of the basic human attitudes
toward life—gallantry and chivalry, respectively—as these are manifested in a more or less contemporary (1900 to 1910) Southern
milieu. They are comedies, or perhaps more accurately satires of
contemporary manners. *Domnei*, on the other hand, is ostensibly a
romance in the medieval manner, but conceived ironically and
enlivened with the somewhat gaudy colors of Pierre Louÿs.

    Compared with the comedies after *The Cream of the Jest* these
comedies of what might be called the middle period lack "gusto,"
a quality which Cabell posits as a necessary ingredient of literature
that endures.[1] They lack also the thematic scope of the later
comedies; they are in fact decidedly mundicidious—not precisely in
the sense that *Gallantry* is so, but mundicidious in that they are
bound to a particular earthly time and place which shapes theme
and style as well as characters. This remains true despite the fact

77

that all three make use of a variety of techniques designed to suggest the possibility of finding a broader and more general significance in the action.

All three comedies do, however, show marked gains in maturity of interest and technique: in each there is, besides the multiplicity of superficial ironies, a fundamental underlying irony which, so to speak, emerges to envelope the whole action; and in each Cabell is less concerned with gesture and attitude in themselves and is more deeply concerned with the psychology that lies behind the gesture. And when the three are considered together, they reveal a significant though as yet slight drift toward the use of folklore materials and motifs.

The earliest written of the three comedies is *The Cords of Vanity* (1909), whose subject matter is the callow philanderings of Robert Etheridge Townsend. It is another story of gallantry but of gallantry in its personal, hedonistic aspect (at one time Cabell considered subtitling it "A Picaresque Romance of Hedonism"). It is, to be accurate, the story of a young man's attempt to play for his own half-guessed-at reasons the gallant in an ungallant world. Consequently, while it lacks the scope of action of *Gallantry,* it does escape the conventional formulizations upon which Cabell had depended in presenting gallantry in its eighteenth century setting, and at the same time it does probe far more deeply into the psychology of at least one gallant character. Moreover, *The Cords of Vanity* is the first of Cabell's comedies which is fundamentally ironic in theme and point of view and not merely in style.

In this book Cabell again used a technique which he had adopted to little purpose in *The Eagle's Shadow*—that of telling the story from the point of view of a character who looks back with eyes of relatively greater maturity upon earlier events in which he was involved. Robert Townsend tells his own story: maturity looks upon and appraises the self-important and self-conscious antics of youth. The result is a sort of romantic irony but romantic irony largely free from bitterness or mockery. For the Townsend who narrates the story of his own youth has remained the supreme egotist, a fact of which he apparently is only slightly aware. He mentions casually that he writes from the same itch for self-exposure which presumably motivated Samuel Pepys and Jean-Jacques Rousseau,[2] but he does not seem to realize that such an itch argues a profound egotism, assuming as it does that the personal emotions and attitudes of the writer are important and interesting. Thus, though time has brought Townsend a relatively more sophisticated point of view from which to evaluate his own youth, his primary response is merely sympathetic amusement, and he leaves the fundamental irony of the story inexplicit.

The young Townsend is not only an egotist but the first of the nympholept characters of which Jurgen is the apotheosis. The nympholept theme, however, as it is developed in this novel has none of the metaphysical and psychological implications which it was later to acquire. The basis of Townsend's nympholepsy is substantially different from the basis of Jurgen's. Townsend's series of abortive love affairs represents not so much a search as a flight, a flight from, after all, quite ordinary women whose personalities he does not even come close to understanding. Moreover, despite the presence of the Helen of Troy motif in the story,[3] Townsend is not conceived of as motivated by a vision of unattainable purity and beauty; the psychological basis of Townsend's nympholepsy is fear, specifically fear of the disillusionment and pain which are the liability of a firm commitment to anyone or anything. "Never," says Townsend, "in my life have I been able to endure the contact of unhappiness."[4]

The Helen of Troy motif, as a matter of fact, appears in a context which degrades it to a mere adjunct of Townsend's self-conscious pose as a romantic searcher after beauty. It comes into the story as a convenient entrée for another affair, and the ironic comment with which it is dismissed suggests that it is after all only the by-product of a somewhat adolescent cleverness: " 'Through countless ages I, like every man alive, have followed her [Helen], and fought for her, and won her, and have lost her in the end, but always loving her as every man must do. And I prefer to think that some day—' But my voice here died into a whisper, which was in part due to emotion and partly to an inability to finish the sentence satisfactorily. The logic of my verses when thus paraphrased from memory, seemed rather vague."[5]

Consequently, the fundamental irony in *The Cords of Vanity* does not lie, as it does in *Jurgen,* in the fact that the search for ideal beauty and purity has no object in the real world and only leads roundabout to the fulfillment of man's probable biological and social roles. It lies rather in the fact that Townsend's hedonistic determination to avoid unhappiness dooms him to being always haunted by the suspicion that he has somehow missed the means of achieving happiness. Townsend feels, at least vaguely, that he is being made the butt of some supernal joke: "Heine was right; there is an Aristophanes in heaven" runs as a motif through the novel. But Townsend does not grasp the nature of his own vulnerability, and it isn't until after Charteris has been shot to death as the result of a simple case of mistaken identity (Charteris being mistaken for Townsend) that Townsend partially comprehends the meaning of Elena's enigmatic reply to his peace offering. On the back of a photograph she had written: "His has been the summer air, and the sunshine, and the flowers; and gentle ears have listened to him, and gentle eyes have been upon him. Let others eat his honey that please, so that he has had his morsel and his song."[6] The knowledge that honey may be bitter deters him from tasting, and not having tasted he must forever wonder if it might not have been sweet after all.

This main theme—the dilemma of a hedonism based on fear—is compounded with another, an equally ironic and so far as the development of Cabellian comedy is concerned, far more significant theme. Despite Townsend's trifling and his philandering, he is all the while drifting toward the sensible, motherly Bettie Hamlyn. Townsend's pose of boyishness cannot protect him from her; rather it makes him more vulnerable to her maternal tolerance and affection. In retrospect it is not difficult to see that Bettie belongs in the company of Dame Niafer and even of Maya of the Fair Breasts whom Gerald Musgrave was to encounter upon Mispec Moor; Bettie is clearly one of the lesser servitors of Aesred, the goddess of many aspects, and her role in *The Cords of Vanity* marks the emergence—at least into the twilight world of the partially articulated—of what might be called the Penelope theme. Like Homer's Penelope, Bettie sits patiently at home spinning her web which, as

Townsend partly guesses, has for him an "arachnean aspect." Moreover—again in retrospect—Bettie's violent antipathy to John Charteris (in this comedy a Mephistophelean character) vaguely prefigures the forever inconclusive contest between Aesred and the incorrigible spirit of romance with which all men are more or less infected, a contest that is sometimes in the foreground and always in the background of the later allegorical comedies.

All in all, however, *The Cords of Vanity*—despite the foreshadowings and loomings which, using the later comedies as touchstones, may be discovered in it—remains within the restricted field of the comedy of manners. The important motifs and themes which it may be said to introduce are all thoroughly assimilated to the character and experience of Townsend and are not, therefore, clearly referable to the finite predicament in which all men are involved. For Townsend is presented as particular rather than representative; the device of presenting the story as an intimate confession impresses upon the reader the sense of particularity at the very outset. At the same time Townsend seems scarcely detachable from the carefully dated literary and social milieu of which he is a product.

Moreover, not only is Townsend's particularity stressed but his callowness and superficiality as well; the result is that whatever is assimilated to his character and experience takes from them the taint of triviality. Ostensibly Townsend's attitude is in some sense a gallant attitude, but Townsend's gallantry is a jejune and timid sort, even as compared to the theatrical gallantry of Ormskirk and certainly as compared to that of Jurgen who will taste any drink once and who, if he leaves the scene as puzzled as when he arrived, does nonetheless adventure in all the realms of romance. Its natural expression is not skepticism but a carefully cultivated boyishness which excuses one from the responsibilities of mature thought and action. It is the gallantry of a man who takes nothing seriously because he is incapable of taking anything seriously except as it serves as an adjunct of his own ego.

For example (as the reader learns toward the end), Townsend, like Jurgen, has encountered Pan; he has not, to be sure, come face to face with "the Brown Man," but he has heard his voice speaking through Schopenhauer. "What if," Townsend speculates, "that obsolete notion of Schopenhauer's were true after all—that love is a blind instinct that looks no whit toward the welfare of the man and woman it dominates, but only to the equipment a child born of them would inherit? What if, after all, without variation, love tends to yoke the most incompatible in order that the average type of humanity may be preserved? Then the one passion which all my finest magazine stories teach us to esteem as sacred would be simply the deranged condition of any other beast in rutting-time. Then we, with pigs and sparrows, would be just so many pieces on the chessboard, and our evolutions would be just a friendly trial of skill between what we call life and death."[7] But Townsend does not share Jurgen's passionate need for denial. For ultimately Townsend does not take Schopenhauer any more seriously than he does anything else. It may be that Schopenhauer's view is the acid that has eaten away the substantial foundation of his life, but insofar as it enters into his conscious thought, it merely serves to feed a convenient cynicism, to stand as an axiom upon which he may build his justification for jilting Avis Beechinor.

In matters of theme and motif, the next of Cabell's comedies, *The Rivet in Grandfather's Neck*, written during the years 1910 to 1912 and first published in 1915, is far less richly prophetic than *The Cords of Vanity*. It does, however, extend the use of at least two techniques which were first exploited in the earlier comedy and which are of interest as indications of the growing complexity of Cabell's ironic viewpoint and of his gradual discovery of the usefulness of fairytale and folk-tale techniques and materials. The first and least important of these is the technique of creating an ironic perspective upon the action by using brief summary allusions to current fads, to the big news stories and the topics of national and international speculation of the time. These were the august concerns of the day, and they form a background of events against which the action of the comedy takes place but with which it has no vital relationship. In *The Cords* Cabell used the device as a means of underscoring Townsend's egotistical self-absorptions; in *The Rivet* it proved a useful means of satirizing the provincialism and willful isolation of the South. "At a very remote period, when

. . . according to the fashion notes, 'the godet shirts and huge sleeves of the present modes' were already doomed to extinction; when the baseball season had just begun, and some of our people were discussing it . . . and yet others were predicting the possible significance of General Fitzhugh Lee's recent appointment as consul-general to Habana: at this remote period, in the April of 1896, Lichfield talked of nothing except the Pendomer divorce case."[8] So begins *The Rivet,* but here, as in *The Cords,* the irony is at least double-edged. Though these references to current topics and events indicate that the world is larger than the characters of the comedy assume, yet the way in which Cabell jumbles together fads, gossip, and history serves to point up the ultimate lack of distinctive importance even in these once supposedly vital subjects. Some of these topics once demanded and got pre-eminent notice, but though they may have appeared for the moment main strands in the web of destiny, in the end they scarcely colored, let alone altered in any essential way, the comedy of human existence in which the Pendomers and Musgraves and Townsends participate as fully as the McKinleys and the General Fitzhugh Lees. What is finally suggested is that the "evil" effect of Southern provincialism lies not in the fact that it isolates the Southerner from the important doings of the great world, but in the fact that it encourages him to take himself altogether too seriously.

Far more important, however, than this simple device for establishing an ironic perspective is Cabell's use in both stories—the most "realistic" of his comedies—of the allegorical fairy tale as a means of focusing the theme. The fairy tale used in *The Cords of Vanity,* entitled "The Foolish Prince," is an original clearly done in imitation of Hans Christian Andersen, but touched by the gaudy coloring and somewhat effete aestheticism of the late nineteenth century decadents.[9] That used in *The Rivet in Grandfather's Neck* is the well-known Andersen fairy tale, "The Shepherdess and the Sweep."[10]

"The Foolish Prince" is, so far as the record shows, Cabell's earliest attempt at allegorical fantasy. Compared to the allegorical fantasy of *Jurgen* and of *Something About Eve,* this first attempt is thin, self-conscious, and over-intellectualized. It is a cleverly contrived puzzle which openly calls for interpretation. Moreover, like everything else in the book, the fairy tale and its meaning are subordinated to the personality and experiences of Townsend; yet, despite this subordination, it does function, not only as a means of forecasting the unwritten conclusion of the comedy—the final entry into the Disenchanted Garden—but as a means of qualifying the irony of the main theme by suggesting that there are not one but several points of view from which Townsend's humorous philanderings can and must be evaluated. In the fable the Foolish Prince, who like Townsend refuses to make any firm commitment, choosing instead to spend his day afield chasing prettily colored butterflies, is set off against the Rationalist, a drab epitome of common sense whose dreary calculations lose for him the beauty and joy of the field without gaining anything better or more substantial than what comes to the Foolish Prince when finally he skips into the Disenchanted Garden. Thus, the irony which plays about Townsend's restless dissatisfaction and final return to Bettie Hamlyn is modified by the suggestion that perhaps after all Townsend's way was at least no less fruitful than other more acceptable and common sense ways.

"The Shepherdess and the Sweep" is used to similar purpose—pointing up the theme and multiplying the ironic implications of the comedy; however, the Andersen fairy tale is a far more complex affair. In it there is no simple allegorical equation between action and meaning. It is susceptible to more than one interpretation, and it brings into the story dark ambiguities—for instance, that suggested by the presence of the goat-legged person—ambiguities whose sources are deep in ancient myth and folklore and whose full significance evades Colonel Musgrave's interpretation and whose presence suggests the inadequacy, too, of Patricia's ironic perception that the rivet to which all the little china people must give thanks for the ordered security of their tiny world does nonetheless "keep us stiff-necked against all sorts of calls." "The Foolish Prince" is neatly tailored to fit the action of the comedy; "The Shepherdess and the Sweep" stands, so to speak, independent of and above the comedy and includes it. The characters of the comedy are, to an extent they do not guess, little china people who are protected from a knowledge of their own insignificance by a false tradition, by the lies which they half-believingly tell one another, and by the words which govern their emotions and their actions.

The theme suggested by the fairy tale is a familiar one in Cabellian comedy: man, whatever his aspirations, cannot endure the rarefied atmosphere of his own ideals nor can he endure the truth, and so, though for the moment he may approximate his ideal image of himself and of what his life should be, ultimately he can survive only among the familiar illusions of his conventional world. This in part is also the theme of *The Rivet in Grandfather's Neck*. Rudolph Musgrave is raised to the height of poetry and vitality by his love for Patricia, just as he is raised to the height of magnanimous gesture and self-sacrifice by his pseudochivalrous devotion to Ann Charteris, but in the long run Musgrave can exist only by loyalty to his inherited illusions about himself and his world, and despite appearances there is considerable doubt that he ever even for a moment really escapes from them. The reduplicated love letters that are made to serve many loves, the torrent of frothy rhetoric about the old and the new South that Musgrave delivers upon the slightest pretext, the magnanimous gestures which cannot be denied because they are picturesque— all these things suggest that Rudolph Musgrave does not escape, and they point to the central irony of the comedy. Rudolph Musgrave, who thinks of himself and is thought of as a master of words, is in fact one of those men who in Queen Freydis's phrase are "used by words." His own words and actions are not shaped by his emotions and attitudes, but rather his emotions and attitudes are shaped by words and by what a largely verbal tradition tells him is expected of him. Consequently, he is a man of gestures and poses; the mainspring of every one of his fine acts of self-denial is the simple thought—what a gesture!" And while Musgrave likes to think of himself as stiff-necked against circumstances, in reality he is no more than the perfect expression of the circumstances among which he has lived his life.

For the most part both the humor and the irony center in the character of Rudolph Musgrave, particularly in his blindness, in his failure to discriminate and to grasp the significance of things.

In Rudolph Musgrave's mind many things—his genealogies, his marriage, his chivalrous devotion to Ann Charteris—lie together like items on the front page of a newspaper, without a clearly assigned order of importance; and he, like the reader of a newspaper, assigns importance to these things simply on the basis of what his inherited illusions allow or dictate. The consequence is that he fails to see what his life and the life of his community really come to, though the reader of course sees very clearly.

This situation is essentially of a piece with the basic situation in most of Cabell's comedies, and Rudolph Musgrave is no more deliberately a mountebank than the majority of Cabell's comic protagonists; yet the irony of *The Rivet* is far more caustic than that of any of the comedies which preceded or followed it. Unlike the other comedies it leaves with the reader a distinct residue of acid and gall. The explanation of this difference lies largely in the fact that in this comedy Cabell works more closely and immediately than in any other with his particular contemporary milieu; he evokes realistically a world and a series of experiences in which the reader is sentimentally involved. Consequently the characters of the comedy impose upon the reader their personal sense of waste and suffering, and the fact that Rudolph Musgrave is protected by his illusions from any real awareness of this waste and suffering, for which he is partially responsible, merely serves to sharpen the edge of the irony by suggesting that there is much that is vicious in these, to Musgrave, kindly illusions.

Whereas the protagonists of the later comedies are, for the most part, alone in a world of masks and symbols, Musgrave exists in a world of ordinary human beings who have a mortal stake in his perception or lack of it, whose happiness or unhappiness is partially dependent upon what he is and does; moreover, whereas the protagonists of the later comedies are necessarily blind, and often fortunately so, in the midst of their highly ambiguous experiences, Rudolph Musgrave's blindness, except from a purely selfish point of view, seems unnecessary and in some instances reprehensible. It seems particularly reprehensible, for example, that he fails to see, let alone understand, the dark shadows which Patricia and Virginia cast in his life.

Patricia, despite her petulance and vapidity, draws the reader's sympathy, and consequently her claim upon life to yield her some sort of happiness seems important and not unreasonable. Yet for her there is no compensation. Such sacrifices as she makes are fruitless, and her alternatives—Musgrave or Charteris—are equally unlikely to yield the love which she needs. Caught in an apparently unresolvable dilemma, she is sacrificed without her consent to Rudolph Musgrave's moribund chivalry. That at the end of his life Rudolph Musgrave should then feed and soothe his ego with distorted memories of her impresses the reader, not as a kindly dispensation of illusion, but as a final affront to Patricia's real personality, however shallow that may have been.

As for Virginia, the deeply wronged Negro servant whose "pleasant yellow face" is "as expressionless as an idol"—the effect of her presence in the comedy is not so immediately felt as the effect of Patricia's fate, but ultimately it contributes even more to those undercurrents of feeling which give the comedy its peculiar bitterness. Virginia's presence in the comedy unmistakably indicates that there is a vicious, sinister aspect to the illusions which hedge the lives of Musgrave and his fellow Lichfieldians. It suggests that these illusions do not so much shield them from the dumb malevolence of the universe as they do blind them to specific evils in their midst, evils which their attitudes have created and fostered. Rudolph Musgrave's failure and his community's failure to recognize this, and their generalized and condescending benevolence toward Virginia, constitute both a tacit denial that she has any claim upon their consciences and a refusal or inability to recognize that they themselves are threatened by the living malice and resentment that her mask-like face conceals.

The Rivet in Grandfather's Neck is Cabell's closest approach to what has sometimes been called bitter or dark comedy, and it marks Cabell's farthest advance along the road that leads to the realistic novel of contemporary manners. Other works were apparently projected along this same road. In the essay "Townsend of Lichfield" Cabell speaks of a novel entitled "The Strength of the Hills" in the background of which was "a most regrettable story of embezzlement and incest." The novel was written but then destroyed in 1914. He speaks too of the projected story of Wilhelmina Musgrave, which, he speculates, would have provoked numerous indignant editorials against "this foul slandering of the South's aristocracy," and of a "Townsend of Lichfield" which "was to have dealt with Mr. Townsend's personal observations as to American letters since 1903 and as to life in Lichfield during the same period . . . and was to handle both themes candidly."[12] All these books, however, either failed to be written or were destroyed, and while Cabell was still working on *The Rivet* he started another book which marked out more clearly and accurately the road which he was actually to follow. That book was *Domnei*.

Domnei: A Comedy of Woman-Worship was written from 1910 to 1912 and published in book form in 1913. Ostensibly this comedy is an imitation of medieval romance, and it is indeed Cabell's nearest approach to pure romance in the traditional sense. The story as it appeared in *Harper's* for April, 1911, was practically innocent of both comedy and irony. In the magazine version the action is largely restricted to Demetrios's court and the emphasis falls upon the tropical sensuousness of the scene and upon the testing of Melisaunt (Melicent). Such irony as the story contains consists in Demetrios's ironic evaluation of his own emotions and in the "disillusioning" moment at the end when the dream suddenly becomes the reality and Perion de la Foret must let slip his grasp of the symbol and embrace the flesh, submitting to all the subtle and painful adjustments necessitated by his having suddenly left the rarefied atmosphere of his chivalrous ideals and come to earth. For that moment, before a purely human love can come to fill the gap, Perion feels the sting of the irony which time in conspiracy with his illusions has prepared for him; but except during that moment the chivalrous attitude, which is the mainspring of the action of the comedy, is presented pretty much without qualification.

To the book-length version of *Domnei* published in 1913 much matter was added, and with it more of the light of both wit and irony, but even in this revision the chivalrous actions are presented with relatively little ironic qualification, and the emotions evoked by the chivalric attitude are allowed their full weight, even as the sophisticated, anti-romantic point of view of Demetrios is allowed its full development. At times irony plays about Perion and about the doings of the medieval church, but it does not touch Melicent. Moreover, however foolish and perhaps unrewarding the attitudes of Melicent and Perion may appear in the sight of a cynical and realistic Demetrios, the reader perceives, as Demetrios himself is painfully constrained to admit, that theirs is a divine sort of foolishness which does make them in some sense ideal and admirable people. And Demetrios must ultimately lose, baffled and bewildered by, and somewhat envious of, that sublime foolishness.

Yet, as Demetrios believes and as Cabell less crudely believes, everything in life has a price as well as a value, and idealism is least likely to be excepted from this rule. Part of the price which Perion pays is, of course, that moment of disillusionment that he suffers at the end; this, however, is as it generally is in Cabell's comedies, only a momentary rending of the veil. The real price is one of which neither Perion nor Melicent can ever be fully aware. It is the price which Ahasuerus announces to Melicent when he tells her that though Perion may win her, it is only cynical, disillusioned and sin-stained men such as himself and Demetrios who can fully appreciate the value and the exquisite rarity of her spirit.[13] And this is also the deep, quiet irony which underlies *Domnei* without disturbing the romantic surface.

It is not, however, merely in the very different quality of the irony nor in the fact that it is Cabell's most unqualified attempt to delineate the chivalrous attitude that the story marks a line of development in some ways diametrically opposed to that suggested by *The Rivet in Grandfather's Neck*. It is rather in the fact that *Domnei* points the way and is at least a small step toward the technique of allegorical fantasy. Poictesme had, of course, been discovered during the writing of *Gallantry*, but in that book Poictesme is merely another French province, distinguished from other French provinces only by being fictional and the scene of Ormskirk's temporary rejuvenation. In *Domnei* the symbolic significance of Poictesme is enlarged, though the historical frame and point of view are retained. The story is still treated so as to give the reader the sense of having been carried back to a historical way of life and to a more or less historical place; it remains earth-bound by the pretense of being true to daily human life as someone once lived it. But, nonetheless, in this comedy the boundaries of Poictesme are, so to speak, blurred. Poictesme is less a territory which can be reached by crossing the English Channel and riding to the south as Ormskirk did, and more one in which romantic and legendary things have taken place; it is now the scene of the Melusine romances and the place where domnei exists as something more than a lovely poetic fiction, as a vital determining force in the lives of men. In short, as it develops in *Domnei* Poictesme is much closer to being a place where human living can be adequately rendered in words, actions, and symbols.

Moreover, two of the characters in this comedy of woman-worship, because their very names are charged with symbolic implications, cannot be accounted for simply by the rather mechanical functions which they perform in the narrative. These are the enigmatic Melusine and Ahasuerus. Neither Perion nor Melicent grasps the meaning of these characters or their relationship to what Perion and Melicent do and suffer, nor can the reader grasp these things without the supporting context provided by the rest of *The Biography of Manuel*. With this supporting context, however, it is clear that Melusine and Ahasuerus play a symbolic role in the story of Perion and Melicent, that they not only represent in this comedy Cabell's first excursion into the realm of folklore and the supernatural but his first attempt to use the materials he finds there for symbolic purposes. The technique used is a familiar one to the readers of the later comedies.

Melusine and Ahasuerus are used to personify those drives and those psychological states and experiences which underlie human behavior and which may or may not have their source in the external universe but which man often experiences as if they were something exterior to himself, as if they were forces which acted upon him from without.

Melusine is, in fact, a localized personification of the Witch-woman, who is in turn but a projection of man's dream of a perfection of beauty in the female. In a sense, she is the shadow that man takes for the whole being in that moment when shadow and substance fuse and he gives his love to a woman, or she may be said to stand for the ambiguous relation between beauty and procreation, a possibility suggested by her periodic assumptions of fish or serpentine forms.[14] On the other hand, Ahasuerus, drawn from the widespread legend of the Wandering Jew,[15] symbolizes the eternally wandering, lonely, and dissatisfied human soul. This might be called his general symbolic value; he has also a more specific or limited symbolic value. He is cursed with the knowledge that what men believe in and value, what he must envy them for being able to believe in and value, are illusions. In this respect he symbolizes the fate of the human soul stripped of its sustaining illusions and of its power to believe, and stands in direct contrast to Perion and Melicent. It may be, too, that in this comedy Ahasuerus subsumes the not yet clearly defined character of Horvendile, the erratic spirit of romance.

At any rate, though they never meet, Melusine and Ahasuerus work, each according to his own nature, to bring about the consummation of the love between Perion and Melicent; they cooperate to create between them the apotheosis of chivalrous belief and action, an apotheosis in which they neither share nor find any satisfaction. For they symbolize generally the buried, never more than half guessed at, biological and psychological forces at work behind appearances, shaping the comedy in which, ironically, they *seem* to play but enigmatic and incidental roles. Their presence in *Domnei* serves to generalize the meaning of the comedy by generalizing the experiences of Perion and Melicent.

The year 1916 serves conveniently, if somewhat arbitrarily, as the terminus for what might be called the middle period in the development of Cabellian comedy. In that year with the publication of *The Certain Hour*, Cabell's initial exploration of what he had conceived of as the three basic attitudes toward life was brought to completion, and though the important transitional comedy, *The Cream of the Jest*, had already been written, it was not to be published until 1917.

Looking back from the vantage point provided by familiarity with the comedies published after 1916, it appears that, in addition to the achievement that would have been apparent in 1916, Cabell had in exploring his three attitudes touched upon many of the themes and motifs which were to be developed and made explicit in the later comedies. Even the familiar comic pattern of the later comedies is present—however incompletely and inadequately realized—in *The Cords of Vanity* and, to a lesser extent, in *The Rivet in Grandfather's Neck*. As yet, however, Cabell either had not seen the full implications of the themes and characters with which he worked or had not yet found the necessary means to express his whole meaning; for as yet he had been content to express himself in terms of localized types and of particular historical periods, and these in turn encumbered and limited his point of view.

It may be, of course, that in the comedies up to and perhaps including *The Cream of the Jest* Cabell was, as Allen Tate once maintained, *primarily* absorbed in an almost wholly Southern preoccupation with the psychology of defeat.[16] Certainly Robert Townsend's assiduous though not quite deliberate evasion of commitment and Rudolph Musgrave's instinctive clinging to fine words that substitute for actions and that both protect and blind—certainly these are aspects of such a psychology. And it may be that it is because Cabell was "a Southern writer," reacting with as well as against the South, that he was first drawn to the problem of defeat and of its appropriate psychology. Growing up in the South in the last two decades of the nineteenth century, he could not very well have escaped all involvement in the experience of defeat, and possibly his concept and exploration of the three basic attitudes toward life reflect his involvement in that experience and in the concomitant myth of a poetic, gallant, and chivalrous civilization which had existed in the South before the Civil War. It might even be argued that Cabell's steadily growing concept of the vital role of illusion in human life is a by-product of his contemplation of the unconcealable discrepancy between what the South wanted to believe about itself and its history and what it actually was and had been.

Yet, without rejecting these possibilities, it is important to remember that Cabell was not concerned with the problem of defeat *solely* as a local matter of Southern conditions. For one thing, the stories and the one comedy written before *The Cords of Vanity* (1909) look to literature rather than to the conditions of contemporary Southern life for their models and inspiration, and it may as readily be true that Cabell's literary interests led him to probe the South's particular psychology as that the conditions in the South served as the center from which his literary interests radiated. For another thing, there is considerable evidence that Cabell, like so many late nineteenth and early twentieth century writers, had been touched by the so-called cosmic chill which had nothing essentially to do with the South's predicament but was rather a result of the conflict between traditional humanistic and romantic values and the implications of nineteenth century scientific thought.[17] Then, too, there is the steadily emerging figure of John Charteris, who even in his first appearance is an exotic in the Southern milieu, a stereotyped embodiment of *fin de siècle* moods and attitudes. Charteris's calculated immorality is, to be sure, another aspect of the psychology of defeat, but it is only secondarily the result of conditions in his immediate surroundings. Actually it is of a piece with the behavior of a punished child who petulantly compounds his wickedness because he is bewildered by his inability to be as good as he believes he should be; it is the psychological consequence of Charteris's frustrated and hopeless desire for unqualified spirituality. The nature of Charteris's experience of defeat and the nature of his reaction to it are liabilities of the human spirit in all times and places.

In any event, to assert, as Allen Tate asserted, that Cabell in deserting Virginia for Poictesme cut his roots and thus deprived his later works of vital sap is to take too restrictedly a Southern view of the matter. Whatever Cabell's preoccupation was in the beginning, somewhere along the line he became absorbed in a broader, more inclusive, and complexly ramifying problem—the inevitable defeat of the human spirit in a naturalistic universe. His removal to Poictesme was far less a flight from Virginia and its particular experience than it was the result of a search for adequate symbols to convey what had come to be his peculiar and non-parochial vision. The bitter irony of *The Rivet in Grandfather's Neck* belied that vision which was after all comic, and though Cabell had created characters who were real enough, he had not succeeded in finding any large enough to convey his whole meaning. "I needed," Cabell has said, "a world in which I alone was omnipotent," a world, that is, disentangled from the historical perspective, unencumbered by historical accident, and beyond the realm of special interests and preoccupations, a special kind of world in which a highly generalized view of human existence could be given the concrete, dramatic embodiment of art.

As was pointed out in the discussion of *The Cords of Vanity* and *The Rivet in Grandfather's Neck*, Cabell had in writing those comedies discovered the value of the fairy tale as a means of focusing his themes; and his use of "The Shepherdess and the Sweep" indicates that he had discovered that the fairy tale, for all its apparently naïve fantasy, may penetrate with an unexpected boldness to the core of human experience and human psychology. In writing *Domnei*, or indeed sometime before, he discovered that legend and folklore could yield for symbolic purposes such richly connotative figures as Melusine and Ahasuerus. What in essence Cabell was apparently coming to realize is that legends, folklore, and myth in general, far from being merely fantastic products of a childish mentality, do in fact often express with a peculiar dramatic force what Jung has called "the phenomenology of the spirit."[18] The importance of this discovery becomes clear when we recall that Cabellian comedy depends upon the possibility of viewing the phenomenology of the human spirit from a "disintoxicated" point of view.

In his characteristically whimsical way, Cabell has indicated his own sense of discovery and of its consequences: "It was only [when *The Cream of the Jest* was being written that,] under the guidance of Richard Harrowby, I took up in a more or less serious way the study of what is loosely called 'magic,' and that I learned something of those realities which are behind what we, just as loosely, call 'ordinary experience.' It was only then, in fine, that I turned definitely away from the merely mundicidious." In another place he has recorded his feeling of having come into his own at that time: "In preparing the Storisende edition of the Biography, during 1927-1930, I found all the books prior to *The Cream of the Jest* to have been written by persons who are to me, nowadays, comparative strangers. I edited the entire Biography as best I might. But only in *The Cream of the Jest* and in its temporal successors had I any sense of dealing with my own work."[19]

As has already been suggested, this book is in many ways a transitional comedy. It is a bridge between this world of ordinary experience and that other world which is ambiguously of the mind and imagination and yet a place in itself, a world in which everything is pregnant with meaning and through which man either picks his way gingerly or, with sublime unconcern, stumbles on from unguessed mystery to unguessed mystery. Here Cabell seems to have seen his kingdom clearly but has not yet entered in and taken possession of it.

The Cream of the Jest breaks more completely than any of the preceding comedies, excepting *Domnei,* with the conventional pattern of the comedy of manners. It was originally planned to present a series of Richard Harrowby's adventurings in the occult, "but Saturn very plainly stood in the ascendancy at the scheme's birth; for as these stories came into being, no one of them, save only 'Concerning David Jogram,' met with the then present need of any discoverable magazine. The dizain was therefore abandoned; and of the eight stories finished, some were destroyed, while others were utilized variously. . . . Two of these tales, as they had been written in the spring of 1911, were combined and rewritten in 1913, with addition of considerable new matter, so that before 1914 had well begun to make the world safe for hypocrisy, these stories had blended into one continuous and fairly long Comedy of Evasions, called then *In the Flesh,* but a little later rechristened *The Cream of the Jest.* . . ."[20] Cabell had already, in 1910, ventured into the occult with "Concerning Corinna"—a Poesque tale about the seventeenth century poet Herrick who, in the tale, is represented as having penetrated the veil of karma and come face to face with those deep subterranean forces of life at the price of madness and suicide.[21] Whatever intervened during the following years to put Cabell's mind on a somewhat different tack is not clear, but *The Cream of the Jest,* as it was finally published in 1917, is a very different book from what was apparently at first intended. It is, rather than a book of occult adventurings, a book of adventurings in the kingdom of the mind, Felix

Kennaston's mind, and it contains only subdued overtones of the occult.

The reader of this Comedy of Evasion finds himself suspended between two worlds, neither of which can in any ultimate sense be called *the* real world except by courtesy of convention. One of these is the world of ordinary experience. The other is an idealized dream world penetrated by Felix Kennaston with the aid of the spurious Sigil of Scoteia. Both worlds as Kennaston early comes to realize are worlds of impenetrable illusion, differing only in that the world of ordinary experience is defined by habit and convention while the other world is fashioned by the inborn yearning of man for a place "wherein human nature has kept its first dignity and strength; and wherein human passions are never in a poor way to find expression with adequate speech and action."[22]

The immediate source of humor and irony in *The Cream of the Jest* is the contrasting interplay of these two worlds. The commonplace world in which Kennaston lives with his friends and neighbors is presented in a series of small domestic comedies, and naturally and appropriately enough the comedy of this world is the comedy of inadequacy; greatness is made to go in the tattered rags of worn-out clichés, talent rises on the wings provided by prurience and fad, and all conversation, however intimate the situation, runs in the barren gulches of the conventional and expected. The general inadequacy which is exposed by these comic techniques is boldly underscored by constant juxtaposition with that other world in which speech and action are always commensurate with the occasion, whether of good or evil, joy or sorrow. The actual embodiment which Cabell gives that other world in this comedy consists of many brightly colored fragments of historical romance.

Clearly this is not yet Cabell's mature manner, the manner of *Jurgen, Figures of Earth,* and *Something About Eve,* which forces the reader to enter a world that is frankly fantastic and alien yet symbolically the real home of the human psyche. The method of *The Cream of the Jest* is only in part dramatic and only in small part symbolic. By and large, it is discursive. The reader shares Kennaston's experiences, but the meaning of those experiences is to a large extent given in Kennaston's discursively elaborated meditations and in the digressive commentaries of the narrator, Richard Harrowby.

Nonetheless, this transitional comedy does decidedly point the way to the allegorical and symbolic comedies that are to follow. For one thing, though in the earlier comedies the reader is made aware that the characters are beset by illusions and that in consequence they misinterpret themselves and their world, he at the same time is made to feel, because of the relatively realistic treatment and because his vision is wider than that of any character, that his own perceptions are firmly and properly rooted in the real world of ordinary experiences; this is not quite so distinctly true of *The Cream of the Jest*. To be sure, the constant suggestion that the world in which Kennaston finds Ettarre is merely a private dream world allows the reader to retain a more or less normal orientation; yet the comedy in statement, if not in form, challenges all of the common workaday assumptions about the nature of reality. For another thing, it is in *The Cream of the Jest* that the comic pattern characteristic of the later comedies is first clearly articulated, though not in its final terms.

Felix Kennaston does not, himself, know how to classify the world which is opened to him by the mysterious power of the Sigil of Scoteia—whether as a private dream world or as a world of occult realities. It may be mere dream stuff, the flimsiest fantasies of an overheated imagination. Yet if reality is to be judged by vividness of impression and by the quantity and quality of felt life, then this dream world is the more real; it is at any rate, Kennaston comes to feel, more aesthetically satisfying. For though such experiences as Kennaston has in it are fragmentary, they are, so far as they go, fully realized: they are rendered with an adequacy of speech, action, and emotion, emotion which Kennaston may savor without being overwhelmed. In this dream world Kennaston always has the deeply satisfying feeling that he is larger than the situations in which he figures, that he somehow includes them rather than is included in them.

With Kennaston aesthetic considerations come first as the basis of value and ultimately even of religion and morality, and consequently the much greater aesthetic satisfaction to be had in the dream world as well as the presence in that world of Ettarre, the epitome of feminine loveliness and desirability, leads Kennaston more and more to abandon himself to it. His true interest is poured into it, and he accepts sardonically or with half-amused resentment the fact that this dreaming being must be concealed in an unprepossessing body and subjected to a "life made up of unimportant tasks and tedious useless little habits."[23] Moreover, his adventurings in the dream world provide him with a perspective upon the world of commonplace experience which at first intensifies his sense of alienation from that world. Moving at random through historical time and observing men at their work and play, Kennaston is driven to the conclusion that "everywhere men had labored blindly, at flat odds with rationality, and had achieved everything of note by accident," and that "life was not a part of the universe at all perhaps, but, rather, an intruder into the cosmic machinery."[24]

In time, like Jurgen, Kennaston comes uncomfortably to feel that man, in the flesh, is the butt of some complex and multiform cosmic jest. Man is a creature of dreams, yet he is doomed to parody his real self and to travesty his dreams in his corporeal actions. Man is obsessed with the ideals of courage and beauty and purity symbolized in the vision of Ettarre, yet nowhere may he find these things tangibly realized, never may he touch Ettarre. Man feels sharply his own loneliness and longs for companionship, yet it is impossible for him to achieve vital and intimate communication with any other human being. Man longs, or believes he longs, for truth, for a knowledge of reality, yet his only means of getting any information whatever about reality is through his five exceedingly fallible senses.[25]

These are the multiple forms of the jest, and these are the somewhat "dusty truisms" with which not only Felix Kennaston but also Jurgen and Manuel and Gerald Musgrave must come to terms. All of these truisms, when grasped emotionally in their full implication, point the way to naturalistic despair. However, what is said of Ettarre might equally well be said of man, as Cabell understands him—the ways of his elusions are many.

The most obvious means open to Kennaston of eluding the consequences of his "knowledge" is that of clinging tenaciously to his dream world and, so far as possible, letting the other go. But though his thought verges at times upon solipsism, he is basically dissatisfied with the curiously divided life which he finds himself living, and this dissatisfaction drives him toward the elaboration of a personal and eccentric philosophy by means of which he transcends his axiom-based skepticism and reattaches himself to real life as his fellow beings understand the term. Pondering the fragments of human history that he has been privileged to witness, Kennaston can discover no rational plan, no discernible plot; yet everywhere, he finds, there is a persistent striving. What all life seems to be striving toward and what all men seem to yearn for, Kennaston decides, is that "life might become symmetrical, well-plotted, coherent, and as rational as living is in books." By this dubious by-way, Kennaston arrives at the concept of life as artist, of life as comparable to a romancer spinning an endless romance and striving ceaselessly for the perfection of art. Perceiving that even apparent symmetry exists nowhere in nature except in the figure of man, Kennaston reclaims on purely aesthetic grounds man's ancient sense of himself as the crown of creation. From this way station Kennaston moves on to the concept of God as artist and of the crucifixion as God's masterpiece, and from its contemplation he draws his own deepest satisfaction. When translated into aesthetic terms, the mysteries of the Christian church become acceptable to Kennaston, and through a back door, plainly marked unorthodox, he enters unsuspected into the church and makes "the image of Christ his own."[26]

In time Kennaston also comes to suspect that there is a vital though hidden link between his dream world and the world of ordinary experience. Not only does he surprise the look of Ettarre in the eyes of Muriel Allardyce, but he is told by Ettarre, herself, "All women resemble me. . . . Whatever flesh they may wear, and however time-frayed or dull-hued or stained by horrible misuse that garment may seem to be, the wearer of that garment is no less fair than I, could any man see her quite clearly."[27] When Kennaston later discovers what he supposes to be the missing half of the Sigil of Scoteia on his wife's bathroom press, he is convinced, despite the absence of any sign of recognition on her part, that she is in some mysterious way identified with Ettarre—Ettarre become flesh and possessed, though unrecognized, by him. The effect of this supposed revelation is to cast a nimbus of mystical suggestion about all human, fleshly ties, to endow them with un-guessed depths of meaning and beauty. "I was happier," says Kennaston, "than I had ever been in any dream . . . I saw that the ties of our ordinary life here in the flesh have their own mystic strength and sanctity. I comprehended why in our highest sacra-ment we prefigure with holy awe, not things of the mind and spirit, but flesh and blood. . . . A man and his wife, barring stark severance, grow with time to be one person, you see; and it is not so much the sort of person as the indivisibility that matters, with them."[28] This mystical glow obviously cannot endure full daylight, but it brings to Kennaston—at a price—a depth of serenity and contentment that can never be wholly dissipated. The price is that Kennaston, an author, writes no more books, for having dis-pensed with the need for his dream world, he has dispensed, too, with the need to write books.

At the end of the comedy, the exact nature of Kennaston's ex-periences and their value, except in terms of his personal satisfaction and contentment, are left apparently ambiguous. The Sigil of Sco-teia turns out to be only a portion of a discarded top of a cold-cream jar, and the whole of Kennaston's seemingly occult privileges and adventurings, it develops, can be explained as a case of self-hypnosis induced by the bright glare of the small object. This natural expla-nation is at odds with Kennaston's feeling—a feeling which the read-er to some extent shares with him—that these experiences open out upon "those realities which are behind what we call ordinary experi-ence." The ambiguity here, however, is not quite so irresolvable as it may appear to be. The possibility of hypnosis, taken with one or two other hints in the text, suggests that though Kennaston has not opened any forbidden windows on the real world, he has with the aid of the spurious Sigil and of his own active imagination pene-trated into the depths of his own psyche and there stumbled upon some general truths.

The possibility of such an interpretation would seem to be suggested by Richard Harrowby's comment upon the occult: "As touches what we call the 'occult,' delusion after delusion has been dissipated, of course, and much jubilant pother made over the advance of knowledge. But the last of his delusions, which man has yet to relinquish, is that he invented them. This too must be surrendered with time; and already we are beginning to learn that many of these wild errors are illegitimate children of grave truths. Science now looks with new respect to folk-lore."[29] If Kennaston's delusions are neither visions or hidden realities nor in any sense creations of his own, then they must arise out of the depths of his unconscious life. The grave truths referred to are, of course, truths of the human psyche, and the respect which science grants to folklore is by way of recognizing in them the indirect expression of the phenomenology of the spirit, the projection and dramatization of the adventures of the psyche.

The suggestion, then, is strong that Kennaston's occult adventures are to be viewed in some such light as this. In penetrating to the depths of his own psyche Kennaston discovers his identity with Horvendile, the romantic demiurge who is after all only the personification of the spirit of creativity in which Kennaston, as an author, participates more fully than most men, but from which no man is wholly excluded. He unearths, too, the deep-buried image of *the* wholly beautiful and desirable woman, Ettarre. Ettarre, as Kennaston in part comes to recognize, is a highly ambiguous figure. She is bound in an eternally unconsummated yet mysteriously fruitful union with Horvendile—a union symbolizing the ever unfulfilled yearning for the perfection of art and for the ideal generally. The moments of history in which Kennaston participates—moments evoked with a perfection of emotion and gesture, yet left incomplete —further symbolize the results of this union. At the same time, Ettarre is linked both with every woman and with the many-aspect goddess of love, fertility, and earth. The former link is pointed out by Ettarre herself; the latter is clearly indicated in the chapter entitled "Economic Considerations of Piety" in which Kennaston sees the Sigil of Scoteia upon the forehead of the Egyptian goddess, Isis. Ettarre, then, serves both life (sex and fertility) and art; at this level of the psyche all of these disparate urges and images, because of their complex interrelationships, blur into one. Kennaston is at play, though he does not know it, with the fundamental forces of his own psychic life and thus of life itself.

The underlying irony in *The Cream of the Jest* lies in this—that Kennaston, for all his anxious theorizing, fails to grasp the true nature of his experiences and of his dream-world playfellows and that the philosophy which he develops in order to account for and, in a sense, to transcend these experiences is purely personal and eccentric: like the philosophies of all men, it is shaped from within by Kennaston's predilections and most deeply cherished values and in no way reveals the structure of the universe. The reader is privileged to perceive the fallacy, though Kennaston does not; the reader is, in fact, driven to the perception by the opposed point of view of the narrator, Richard Harrowby, who remains skeptical of, and even hostile toward, Kennaston's notions. Still, the reader is forced to see that, far from being harmful, Kennaston's fallacies are positively serviceable to him. For his curious metaphysics does make possible his acceptance, with relative ease and contentment, of the finite predicament. It makes possible his acceptance of man's role as fool in the cosmic drama, and it re-enforces the "ordinary ties of the flesh" by suggesting to Kennaston that these are everywhere tinged with the mysterious and the miraculous.[30] Put in another way, it enables Kennaston to evade the consequences of his "knowledge"—those dusty truisms which point the way to despair.

For the reader who comes to *The Cream of the Jest,* after reading the rest of the Biography, the statement Harrowby makes near the end—"It occurred to me that his history was, in essentials, the history of our race, so far"[31]—carries a significance beyond that immediately developed by Harrowby himself. Such a reader understands without prompting that there is nothing either ultimate or unique in Felix Kennaston's thoughts and experiences. Through his meditations echo the queries and laments of Manuel, his remote thirteenth century ancestor, and as he himself is forced reluctantly to admit, Kennaston is but the fleshly garment which Horvendile for the moment wears, and Horvendile in turn is but one aspect of the life force which, if not eternal, is at least diuternal. At the same time, such a reader sees in Kennaston's thought and experience another tribute to that ingenuity, that vanity, that inveterate habit of substituting illusion for fact and logic, by means of which the human spirit contrives to endure.

The comic pattern which emerges clearly for the first time in *The Cream of the Jest* was to remain the essential comic pattern of the later comedies. This pattern as the comic protagonist experiences it consists basically of three steps or movements: first, the felt awareness in various terms of the finite predicament, that is, of the humanly irremediable condition of incompleteness and imperfection; second, the struggle against the limitations implied in the finite predicament; and third, the acceptance of the human condition as, for all its limitations, upon the whole satisfactory. The third step is fairly complicated, involving acquiescence in the mystery of being as well as the reasonably complacent perception that however radically defective in some respects, the conditions of human living do nonetheless provide for both practical security and poetic beauty. From the reader's point of view the pattern is one of almost instinctive evasions by means of which the comic protagonist protects his ego against the corrosive, disillusioning truths which his struggle forces upon him and by means of which, also, he provides for his own more or less happy ending.

However, as has been pointed out, though the essential pattern remains the same, the comic technique and point of view used in the later comedies is considerably different from that used here. The method of *The Cream of the Jest* seems decidedly timid and tentative as compared with that of the major comedies to follow, the mature comedies in which Cabell boldly adopted the perspective and conventions of folklore and myth. Whereas the world in which Kennaston enjoys his occult adventures is not the familiar world yet is recognizably and immediately derived from it, the world of *Jurgen* and the succeeding comedies is almost wholly fabulous and mythical, a world controlled by sorcery and largely emancipated from the normal conditions of time and causality. Moreover, whereas in *The Cream* Kennaston's dream world, which reflects symbolically the hidden forces of his own psyche, is juxtaposed to a public, conventionally accepted world, in the comedies that followed these two world become so blended as to be indistinguishable. It becomes next to impossible to designate those things which belong to the mind of the protagonist and those things which are exterior to that mind. For while the protagonist conceives of himself as moving through an objectively present world in which he encounters ambiguous beings distinct from himself who baffle, threaten, and invite him, in actual fact many of these beings personify forces—drives and desires—which properly speaking are at work within him, though they are not merely personal to him. At the same time, the inevitable wives of the protagonists lose their individuality, merging into a single archetype that includes not only all wives but potentially all women. Thus, in the succeeding comedies Felix Kennaston's awareness that no man can—at least as a flesh-and-blood being—get beyond the boundaries of his own mind is rendered dramatic, and not merely a portion but the whole of the comic protagonist's experiences become allegorical and symbolic.

That Cabell, having perceived that the apparent errors of folklore are the illegitimate offspring of gravest truths, should be attracted to the methods and materials of folklore and myth is not surprising; his own world-view, while built upon certain ontological assumptions about the nature of the universe, is primarily concerned with the phenomenology of the human spirit. For this is the only reality with which man has any assured contact. Of course, however much Cabell may look to the methods of folklore and myth, his comic fantasies remain sharply distinguished from that source by his sophisticated intention. That is, whereas folk tales and myths (if we follow the interpretation of Carl Jung) are spontaneous, archetypal expressions of the unconscious life of the psyche, Cabell's comedies make use of methods and materials drawn from these sources for the purpose of expressing Cabell's self-conscious interpretation of the adventures of the human psyche as viewed from a preconceived metaphysical point of view, in other words, to render what has already been analyzed. Thus, while folklore and myths are characterized by spontaneous and ultimately irreducible symbols (archetypes), Cabell's comedies tend to allegory —thus, also, the detachment, the irony, the laughter which are largely foreign to these sources.

7

The Late Comedies

       Jurgen, published in 1919, was the first of Cabell's comedies written in what we may call his mature style and from his mature point of view; after *Jurgen* no further significant development takes place. It would, of course, be possible to talk about a "late" style—the style, that is, of *The Music From Behind the Moon* of 1926, *The White Robe,* of 1928, and *The Way of Ecben* of 1929. These stories are dominated by theme and are presented with a severe economy of detail and of connotation, and in a highly intellectualized, relentlessly allegorical style. They were, however, conceived to bridge a felt gap in the Biography,[1] and it is at least conjecturally possible that their self-conscious, formalized allegory reflects not so much growth as the pressure and strain of necessity. At any rate, in his later writings—for example in the trilogy, *The Nightmare Has Triplets* (1934-37)—Cabell returned to a technique and a style which in all essentials are like those of *Jurgen* and of the other major comedies in the Biography.

       The major comedies—*Jurgen* (1919), *Figures of Earth* (1921), *The High Place* (1923), *The Silver Stallion* (1926), and *Something About Eve* (1927)—are all of a type. This is not to say, as numerous reviewers and critics have said, that these comedies are repetitious. The charge of repetitiousness betrays either a superficial reading which is impressed only with such common techniques as displacement and double-entendre or a reading which grasps only the broad pattern and none of the nuances or variations. The fact that all of the major comedies are written from the same point of view should forestall any surprise over the fact that the essential pattern remains the same. Moreover, it should be remembered that for the comic writer in general and for Cabell in particular all human experience is at bottom probable and therefore undifferentiated. The unity of human experience, however, does not preclude the possibility of variety, for though human experience is broadly uniform and normative, it has many facets. Each of Cabell's major comedies takes up a different facet, elaborates a closely related but different theme; each refers to and contributes to the same core meaning but it does not exhaust that core meaning. In other words, while Jurgen and Gerald Musgrave confront a similar world and endure a similar fate, their comedies do not repeat one another; their comedies taken together make a larger and more complex statement than does either taken separately.

What first and most forcefully impresses itself upon the reader who comes to the major comedies after having read the earlier comedies is the marked gain in gusto, due primarily to the broad comic treatment of sexuality and to the ever increasing dependence upon often recondite folklore materials. As outstanding as these things are, however, they are only secondary characteristics; the primary characteristics, those which are essential to the definition of Cabellian comedy as something distinct, are the peculiar qualities of the fantasy world in which the comedies take place, discussed in the preceding chapter, and the unorthodox character—or perhaps more accurately, situation—of the comic protagonist.

In several respects the comic protagonist's situation is similar to that of the typical hero of folktale or fairy tale: he is a quester, a searcher in the wonderful; his goal often takes the objective form of the unattainable princess; and he finds himself thrown into relationship with superhuman figures who ambiguously help and hinder him in his quest. Now generally speaking, the typical folk-tale or fairy-tale hero, despite his often unqualified success, is far removed from the typical hero of comedy. It is true, of course, that many folk and fairy tales might conceivably be treated as primitive comedies inasmuch as in the end the hero triumphs over all obstacles and attains to a normally desirable goal—marriage to the beautiful princess and happiness ever after. This traditional happy ending, however, is no doubt due to the presence of a large measure of wish fulfillment, or—and this comes to much the same thing—if Jung is correct in his analysis, it is a prophecy of an impossible psychic state of wholeness and complete self-possession. Take away the elements of wish fulfillment or prophecy and the situation becomes potentially tragic, the hero potentially a tragic hero. For then the hero's quest becomes the pursuit of an impossible perfection; undertaking the quest, he exposes himself not only to frustration and harm at the hands of an unyielding reality but also to the painful discovery of his own inadequacies and deficiencies. So to speak, he runs the risk of incurring punishment at the hands of the probable, imperfect reality against which he transgresses in his search for perfection, a punishment which takes the form of the agonized contemplation of the dark side of his own nature. For striving after perfection, if sustained, inevitably leads to an ever more acute awareness of all those aspects of the human psyche and those conditions of fate which render perfection an impossibility. Thus, seeking perfection, the hero approaches self-realization; self-realization may be taken as that aspect of the tragic experience which is felt as positive gain, but self-realization cannot be had except at the price of great pain. The tragic symbol of the fully realized self is—again to borrow from Jung—the crucified Christ.[2]

The situation at the opening of each of the major comedies corresponds very closely to the potentially tragic situation described in the preceding paragraph. Jurgen, Manuel, and Gerald Musgrave are, initially, all committed to the hopeless pursuit of impossible perfection. They are animated by a dissatisfaction which leads them to reject the probable norms of human experience and sends them journeying into the wonderful in search of ideal fulfillment and satisfaction. Thus, Jurgen sets out in search of justice, that is, in search of that which will satisfy his deep yearnings for love, beauty, and holiness. Justice in this sense refers simply to the seemingly rational demand that there should be no desire without a corresponding object or that the universe should provide that which is commensurate with man's dreams and in which, consequently, he may find total satisfaction. In Jurgen's case the complex objects of yearning are gathered up and projected in the symbolic figure of Helen of Troy, a variation upon the traditional unattainable princess of folklore. Similarly Manuel, too, is aroused by Horvendile, the spirit of romance, and sent forth in search of another version of the unattainable princess. And Gerald Musgrave sets forth to redeem the mythical kingdom of Antan and, more significantly, to reinstate himself as a god in his appropriate mythology. On first consideration Gerald Musgrave as comic protagonist may appear distinct from Jurgen and Manuel in that Gerald is not consciously in pursuit at any time of the unattainable princess; but it is significant in this connection that Antan, as Maya understood, is inseparable from its ruler, Queen Freydis, and that seen from Mispec Moor the distant hills of Antan assume the appearance of a recumbent female body.[3] The unattainable princess, or the dream woman, in general symbolizes all that the protagonist yearns for—ideal beauty, truth, purity, sanctity, a full-blooded emotional life. She is closely related to the heroine of folklore and is even susceptible to Jungian interpretation as the projected anima of the hero, the symbol of his soul, the possession of which is a necessary condition of complete self-realization.

As rebels against imperfect, probable human experience, then, and as searchers into the wonderful, Jurgen, Manuel, and Gerald Musgrave would seem at the outset to be cast in the traditional role of the tragic hero. There is, of course, no confusion of tone. The appropriate comic tone—the tone of playful detachment—is established at the very beginning of each of the comedies and predominates throughout. *Jurgen* opens with the logical but comic because morally inappropriate defense of the devil; *Figures of Earth* opens with the ironic but humorous miscomprehension of the expression "to make a figure in the world"; *Something About Eve* opens with a mildly satirical treatment of the Southern code of chivalry. This is only to say, however, that the comic intention is declared at the outset. The fact remains that in subject matter, in the situation of the comic protagonist, these comedies trespass upon the domain of tragedy and raise the theoretical problem of how this domain is to be subjugated to the comic spirit.

The practical solution of this theoretical problem lies in the fact that in Cabellian comedy the comic protagonist's character is conceived of not as static but as involved in the general flux; it is both contradictory and mutable. Jurgen, Manuel, and Gerald Musgrave belong neither wholly to the class of the ordinary comic protagonist who is distinct from and opposed to the pariah nor wholly to the class of the tragic hero who is in many respects identical with the pariah. They carry within themselves both the pariah and his opposite; they are neither Faust nor Odysseus but both at once and in sequence. The Faustian component in their make-up is seen in their quest for the unattainable, in their uneasy intuition that they are the dispossessed children of God, and in their general susceptibility to ill-defined desires. It worships Helen and Ettarre and is associated with youth and with youth's romantic dreams and strivings. The Odyssean component is manifested in the healthy sexuality of the protagonists and particularly in the strength of their irrational human ties, their profound susceptibility to the illusions of wife and home. It is associated with domestic sentiment generally and is the natural subject of Maya, goddess of the fertile earth and of worldly wisdom. The Odyssean component is present but for the most part unacknowledged in youth; in middle age it emerges triumphant.

Essentially the influence of the Faustian component upon the character of the comic protagonist is centrifugal, driving him away from the animal center of his being: it forces him into an egotistical revolt against the natural sources and powers from which he lives and so exposes him to the dangers of painful disillusionment and self-knowledge. The Odyssean component clings to the animal center, the animal base, and forms an obscure alliance with the enigmatic Maya (Aesred/Sereda) and the Brown Man (Pan) who from the Faustian point of view represent evil but from the Odyssean are the healthy wisdom of the world of ordinary experience.

In the development of Cabell's major comedies, the Faustian component, like the pariah of Albert Cook's theory of normal comedy, is expelled; it is expelled by time, time being normally the enemy of the tragic protagonist and the friend of the comic protagonist. Of course, the Faustian component and its concomitant mood do not disappear altogether; they linger on as a vague restlessness and as a propensity to play with ideas, but the real power of the Faustian component passes with the passing of youth. The consequent triumph of the Odyssean component is the typical comic triumph of world over spirit, of wisdom, the rule of life, over truth. In the ninth book of the *Odyssey* Odysseus tells Alcinous, "I myself feel that there is nothing more delightful than when the festive mood reigns in a whole people's hearts and the banqueters listen to a minstrel from their seats in the hall, while the tables before them are laden with bread and meats, and a steward carries round the wine he has drawn from the bowl and fills their cups. This, to my way of thinking, is something very like perfection."[4] For Odysseus, in his situation, these things are the promised rewards of expediency and diplomacy, and the statement indicates equally the characteristic mood and the general tendency of the Odyssean component.

To return to terminology previously used—we might say that it is the Faustian component in the comic protagonist which suffers a felt awareness of the finite predicament and revolts against the limitations implicit in it; the Odyssean component makes possible the reconciliation to these limitations. All of this would seem to suggest a degree of inner tension and conflict incompatible with the free play of the comic spirit. Actually, however, in Cabell's treatment this is not the case, for the comic protagonist is generally unaware of his own duality. Only the reader perceives clearly the ironic incongruities and contradictions to which this duality gives rise. The Faustian and Odyssean components within the comic protagonist never really confront one another. Where a confrontation of sorts does take place, it always comes after the decaying Faustian component has lost its power and has come to be felt as something external to and distinct from the personality of the protagonist. Gerald Musgrave does not even recognize the shade of his Faustian youth as it rides past him on its way down to

Antan,[5] and though Jurgen is grieved by his sense of alienation from the image of his boyhood, which he encounters upon the battlements of heaven, he is not aware of any dramatic moment of severance or of any history of struggle.[6] The image of boyhood represents a period and a state of simple faith and innocence in which, if it were permitted, the Faustian component could rest satisfied. On the other hand, while the Faustian mood endures, the comic protagonist does not acknowledge his own Odyssean aspect. He does not admit that there is a part of himself which is preparing to deliver him into the hands of the enemy; instead, he feels himself to be threatened only by powerful and enigmatic beings distinct from himself who would for their own reasons divert him from his goal.

It should be made clear that the ultimate triumph of the Odyssean component over the Faustian does not imply a comparative value judgment. It is the result of a process which happens inevitably in time, and Cabell has shunned all attempt to weigh one component against the other. To do so would be to attempt to make life add up, and life is not—as Robert Townsend points out in the Introduction to *The Cords of Vanity* and as Cabell has elsewhere insisted—a matter of arithmetic. Arithmetic stands both for those habits of mind collectively known as common sense and for the methods and results of science. If one attempts to make life a matter of arithmetic, he exposes himself to the cosmic chill, for the power of arithmetic is a purely destructive magic which exorcises all romantic illusions.[7]

Actually both the Faustian and Odyssean components are equally nourished by illusion—a fact which Manuel discovers when he opens the window of Ageus,[8] which Gerald Musgrave comes to understand after his "son" has marched off toward Antan and Maya has removed his rose-colored spectacles.[9] Moreover, both the Faustian and the Odyssean components have their different but complementary values. The Faustian fills human living with ardent, soul-satisfying illusions and legends which answer to the ageless dreams of sanctity and damnation, purity and justice; and though the Faustian mood is a form of active hybris, to forego it would be to abdicate one's humanity and to accept a life devoid of poetic beauty. If Gerald Musgrave had succumbed to the princess of the first water-gap by the river Doonham (manhood), he would have lost both the ineffable comfort and contentment of Maya's cottage upon Mispec Moor and the rather beautiful ideas with which he delighted to play.[10] The Odyssean component, on the other hand, binds the comic protagonist to the animal center of his being and quietly prepares a final refuge against the destructive implications of the Faustian.

Of course, from the point of view of the primitive psyche whose needs and interests are, in the major comedies, projected in and served by Maya and the Brown Man and their avatars, the inclination of the Faustian component to cut its roots is a distinct threat.[11] In many ways the Faustian component is radically at odds with the primitive psyche and with all its manifestations, for it cannot endure ambiguity or compromise and so would prefer to embrace pure illusion or suffer annihilation rather than see its dreams and aspirations invaded and in a sense appropriated by the animal nature which it wishes to deny.[12]

From the Faustian point of view there is no middle ground; there is only heaven or hell, ideal realization or surrender to the dreadful knowledge of the "two truths,"[13] and in its refusal to compromise with things as they are the Faustian component prepares for the comic protagonist a crushing burden of disillusionment. For the illusions which nourish the Faustian component are evoked by its demands out of the heart of nature and serve, as surely as do the illusions that nourish the Odyssean component, the common needs of the primitive psyche. It is significant in this connection that all of the Faustian illusions are allegorically represented by female figures—Guinevere, Anaitis, Helen, Ettarre. The clear implication of this fact is that the Faustian quest cannot be wholly dissociated from the sex drive, though the supposed objects of the quest in their highly elaborated conscious forms may seem to deny their origin. Furthermore, so far as the Faustian component is concerned all of the lovely personifications of its ideal goals have an arachnean aspect. They are traps set by nature, baits cast before the Faustian rebel with the design of luring him back within the circle of nature. Consequently, whenever the comic protagonist in his Faustian role seems to have won to the woman who offers a substantial fulfillment of his dreams, the woman is almost instantly demoted to the human level, upon which level she imperceptibly blends with the figure of the all-wife.

Varieties of this metamorphosis are encountered throughout *Jurgen, Figures of Earth,* and *Something About Eve,* and everywhere it carries the same implication. These comic *non sequiturs* announce both the uniform ground and the uniform intention of all illusions. This unity of intention and ground is further underscored by the contradictory aspects and ambiguous relationships of the personified powers which confront the comic protagonist. Aesred, in her Sereda avatar, seems flatly opposed to all of the romantic possibilities which may be gathered up into the Faustian component; yet her full-length portrait dominates the library of Cocaigne, and as Cybel she is herself the immaculate goddess of an enthusiastic cult, and through Cybel she is related by extension to Isis and even to Astarte.[14] As Maya of the Fair Breasts—the form she assumes in *Something About Eve*—she is the personification of nature itself, goddess of the fertile and productive earth. In this avatar, too, she appears diametrically opposed to the romantic illusions of the Faustian component; yet as the Mother of Every Princess she stands sponsor to some of these illusions. So far as her complex nature may be reduced to a simple equation, Aesred in her many avatars represents the power of nature to adapt to the demands of the ego on the plane of illusion while persisting in its own more primitive aims.

Consequently, the comic protagonist even in his Faustian role cannot escape from the circle of Aesred's influence: he cannot, whatever his pretensions, avoid subserving the needs and interests of the primitive psyche. All his actions are accordingly touched with duplicity—a fact reflected in the extensive reliance upon double-entendre as a comic technique; and everywhere he suffers a sense of betrayal. From the Faustian point of view life soon becomes treacherous, tragic, impossible.

Fortunately, the Faustian component is never unaccompanied by the Odyssean component. The Odyssean clings to the comic protagonist even in his Faustian role, just as Jurgen's peculiar shadow clings to him throughout his supramundane travels. Jurgen's shadow is, in fact, the shadow of Aesred, that is, of worldly wisdom and experience for which she stands and to which Jurgen is subject in his character as a successful middle-aged bourgeois. Supposedly Jurgen sloughs off this character and re-assumes his Faustian youth, but the power of Aesred, who grants him the gift of youth, is limited. She can grant only the appearance of youth,[15] and so her shadow, which is also the shadow of his former character, clings to him, qualifying all of his experiences and directing him always toward the respectable Odyssean goals of home and wife. Significantly, in the eyes of Merlin, a thoroughly Faustian character, Jurgen's shadow appears a manifestation of the power of evil:[16] from the Faustian point of view everything which is associated with the Odyssean component is seen as belonging to man's lower or darker side, and therefore as having affinities with the power of evil. In *Something About Eve* Maya assumes a shape that is apparently less threatening than her Sereda (Aesred) avatar in *Jurgen,* but the reader is constantly reminded of her malevolent aspect by the variety of domestic animals, once kings and emperors, that graze her pastures. Gerald escapes this meta-morphosis because while the Faustian ceases to be dominant in him, it is present as a makeweight. Its residual presence is ex-pressed in Gerald's unrelinquished belief in his own divinity and in his persistent though increasingly academic interest in Antan and in its inhabitants.

Ironically, however, though the Faustian suffers at the hands of what it conceives to be the power of evil, the cautious wisdom of expediency which Jurgen's shadow in part represents prevents him from arousing the sleeping Helen and from looking too curiously into the arrangements of Heaven,[17] and thereby provides for the qualified survival of two of the illusions by which the Faustian component is nourished. The Faustian component, then, even at the very end is not utterly deposed by the Odyssean but is, so to speak, put upon a strict allowance.

The case of Jurgen, of course, is exceptional, but the power of the latent Odyssean component to work through the Faustian is also variously expressed in *Figures of Earth* and *Something About*

Eve. Manuel, pursuing his restless, imperious, though ill-defined desires, rejects in turn the political power and worldly pre-eminence represented by Alianora, and the power of creativity represented by Freydis, and undergoes thirty years of servitude in the house of the Misery of the Earth in order to redeem Niafer, whom he had originally sacrificed to his Faustian ambitions. That Manuel's sacrifice of thirty years and his subsequent union with Niafer were predestined from the beginning by something fundamental in the character of Manuel is made clear by the fact that upon Vraidex Manuel had preferred Niafer to the Lady Gisele, the unattainable princess, had in fact confused these two symbolic figures. What Niafer actually represents is made equally clear through the means by which she must be redeemed; she stands for common sense—shrewd, worldly wisdom—"the shadow of outlived misery"; thus, she is a servitor of Aesred, she is the prototypical wife and stands in the same relation to Manuel as Jurgen's shadow stands to Jurgen. It is not surprising, then, that almost immediately after her redemption she induces Manuel to set about the conquest of his kingdom—a typically Odyssean undertaking.

Similarly, Gerald Musgrave lingers upon Mispec Moor not so much because of the operation of powers extraneous to himself as because of the growing strength of the Odyssean component within his own nature. Maya makes no overt move to obstruct his journeying toward Antan; to all appearances she is willing enough to see him off. However, the domestic illusions which she builds up about him are deeply satisfying to his Odyssean aspect which under their stimulation emerges in full strength. (Even the thoroughly Faustian Tannhäuser cannot resist the small magic of Maya's rose-colored spectacles.) As with Jurgen, so with Gerald—the Faustian component is put upon an allowance. It is not denied outright, but its claims are deferred from day to day, and gradually it loses its active force and lingers on as a mental habit of playing with beautiful ideas.

What makes this Faustian/Odyssean sequence comic is not merely that it results in the usual comic triumph of the probable norm of human experience but that it makes possible the survival of the human spirit upon terms of reasonable comfort and contentment by forestalling payment of the Promethean debt accumulated by the wayward and rebellious Faustian component. This debt should logically be discharged through suffering, through the assumption of a crushing burden of disillusionment. However, before the comic protagonist in his Faustian role has arrived at this crux, the Odyssean component emerges to dominate his character, and henceforth the Faustian component must live through and in subjection to it. Unlike the Faustian component, the Odyssean always counts the cost; it is too shrewd to risk disillusionment or self-exposure. Except for a singular accident, Manuel would have spent his last years contentedly enough in the Room of Ageus (Usage), and Gerald Musgrave would have spent his upon the porch of Maya's cottage evolving fine theories about the still distantly visible Antan. The comic protagonist in his Odyssean role lives in the spirit of compromise and common sense; he is not wholly immune to the ideals and dreams of his Faustian aspect, but he is content to let them shine in the unmeasured distance. He is cautious and essentially passive, clinging fast to present satisfactions. Furthermore, the illusions which most deeply satisfy him are more serviceable to the primitive psyche because they reflect more immediately its needs and interests—sustenance, the warmth of nest or den, propagation—and therefore they are more stable.

The Odyssean component, then, counterbalances the destructive tendencies and nullifies the tragic implication of the Faustian component. At the same time, it must be remembered that these two components are not purely antagonistic. Both are aspects of the essential human spirit. (Gerald Musgrave who has shed his natural body and travels toward Antan in his spiritual body is nonetheless vulnerable to the Odyssean illusions of family, wife, and home.) And, more important, both serve to evoke a world in which the human spirit can endure. Nature does not particularly care whether man falls victim to the Lady of the First Water-gap or comes to reside upon Mispec Moor, so long as he fulfills his function as a transmitter of the life force; Maya and the Mother of Every Princess are one and the same.[18] However, the preposterous demands and pretensions of the comic protagonist (prepos-

terous in the naturalistic world to which he actually belongs),
and in him the human spirit, force upon natural conditions and
processes spiritual qualities which they by no means possess.
Ultimately, of course, nature has her way with him, but all the
same, like a willful and wayward child he, both in his Faustian
and in his Odyssean roles, draws from her large concessions. She
wishes to claim him as her own and to bend him to her purposes;
she understands, however, that he can be destroyed but not
coerced, and so she produces out of the depth of her own being
those appearances which serve to hold him within the circle of
her power by affording him temporary satisfaction. To be sure,
containing within herself nothing which corresponds to the high-
flown desires of man, she can respond to his demands only with
spurious, illusory gifts; yet, as Gerald Musgrave learns, the value
of these gifts is incalculable.

As Gerald Musgrave sits talking with Abdel-Hareth, who wears
the likeness of his son Theoderick Quentin Musgrave, Gerald
realizes with awed gratitude "from what remote abyss his wife
had drawn the being which seemed his child. . . ." Abdel-Hareth
in his own right, like Jung's archetype, represents, "Vital forces
quite outside the limited range of our one-sided conscious mind; of
ways and possibilities of which our one-sided conscious mind knows
nothing, a wholeness which embraces the very depths of nature.
It represents the strongest, the most ineluctable urge in every being,
namely, the urge to realize itself. It is, as it were, an incarnation
of the inability to do otherwise, equipped with all the powers of
instinct and nature. . . ."[19] And Maya, Gerald realizes, has
coerced this powerful, primordial spirit, which, in so far as she
stands for living nature, is part of her own being, forcing it to
assume the likeness of a child's innocence and helplessness; and
all this she has done because Gerald's own imperious spirit could
not be restrained at a smaller price.[20]

Thus, both the Faustian and the Odyssean components serve,
as it were, to levy a tax upon nature, forcing her to clothe herself
in those appearances which satisfy their need for poetic beauty
and practical security and warmth. The comic protagonist, of
course, can never be fully aware of the game that he plays. He

knows simply that he plays for mortal stakes, and only when the game is more or less played out does he glimpse the facts that it was played without rules and that the prizes offered were not at all what they seemed to be.[21] From the Faustian point of view this state of affairs is tragic; it appears that the comic protagonist is duped out of his divine heritage, a repetition of the ancient story of Esau and the mess of potage. The comic protagonist in his Odyssean role, however, feels that whatever the conditions of the game, he has won a great deal. If illusions and his own blindness have combined to victimize him, they have, he knows, also ministered to his needs; if he is disappointed, he is also grateful.[22] He shrewdly declines the attempt to add up his life[23] and looks about for another place of refuge.

Jurgen, with some regret and much gratitude, bids farewell to the beautiful dream women with whom he has sported and to the dreams which they personify, and returns to his wife, Lisa, about whom he is already busily spinning a lower pitched domestic poetry.[24] Throughout his journeyings in the realms of romance, Jurgen has worn without any inconvenience the shirt of Nessus, symbolizing the malevolent aspect of Mother Sereda's gift, the poisonous, spirit-blasting implications of Jurgen's experiences. Jurgen has worn the shirt without inconvenience because its poison could not penetrate the hard core of his egotistical self-assurance; and at the end, far from renouncing all ideals and dreams as fraudulent because illusory, Jurgen's skeptical and cautious mind, while clinging to the practical comfort and security of a bourgeois home, retains a capacity for genuine reverence for the very real power of man's baseless illusions.[25]

Gerald Musgrave, too, in the end finds that it is to the illusions which have given him his desire that he owes thanks. From the Faustian point of view Gerald's life upon Mispec Moor was a treacherous deception, but Gerald in his Odyssean role understands that upon Mispec Moor under the aegis of compromise life had blossomed into one of its loveliest possibilities. Upon Mispec Moor Gerald had inadvertently, and without ever guessing the whole truth, lived in accordance with the prescription somewhere expressed by Santayana: "I put my hand into [Nature's]. . . . She tells me wonderful tales, but I must never let go her hand lest I become lost in the maze of her invention."

When Gerald with equal inadvertence starts a regression to the primitive and elemental, beginning with the baptism of the Christianized Jehovah with the virility-restoring drops from the Churning of the Ocean and ending with the release of Abdel-Hareth from "the power of the woman," that is, the power of illusion, he brings about the destruction not only of the domestic illusions which Maya has built up about him but the destruction of Antan as well. Yet, Gerald does not repudiate—instinctively knows that he cannot afford to repudiate—his experiences as fraudulent simply because they were unreal; he knows that he has enjoyed all that a rational man can ask for. Moreover, though for the moment Gerald walks "the gray quiet way of ruins," and the world seems so much blown smoke and dust, he soon finds with the aid of Horvendile one last shift by which life may be redeemed. Through the power of the mirror and pigeons—that sacrifice of the birds of Venus, by means of which all the power of love is concentrated upon the small, exclusive image of the self reflected in a tiny mirror, thereby preparing the way for worldly eminence—through this power Gerald repossesses his natural body and finds himself a world-renowned scholar of anthropological sex lore. Thus, instead of submitting to the humiliating simplicity of the "two truths," he forces them to serve as the basis of his personal amusement and worldly fame.

Of course there is satire in this. Cabell is clearly suggesting that the modern scientific interest in sex is the last desperate shift of the spiritually bankrupt. Incidental satire is common in the later comedies. Sometimes it is thoroughly assimilated to the main development of the comedy, as it is here; sometimes it is obtrusive, as it is in the satire upon democracy in the chapter "As to Applauded Precedents" of *Jurgen*.

Even Manuel, for all his dissatisfaction and bewilderment, elects when an alternative is offered to stand by those illusions by which he has lived in his old age, though to do so means his death. Manuel differs from Gerald Musgrave and Jurgen in that his conscious mental processes are relatively unimportant; he lives through obligations, irrationally assumed, and finds his partial fulfillment only in action.[26] In other words, Manuel is closer than Jurgen or Gerald to the inarticulate, impelled, and unconscious average of human life. At the same time, Manuel's rise from the position of swineherd to that of the ruler of Poictesme recapitulates allegorically man's development beyond unconscious identity with the elemental forces of life. As swineherd Manuel is symbolically associated with Proserpina, who stands for the dark hidden forces of life and to whom swine are sacred. This association is re-enforced by the fact that Manuel's putative father is the blind swimmer, Oriander, and that at the beginning of his comedy Manuel is under the spell of a fairy mistress, Suskind, who apparently stands for the deep longing of the blood which is at bottom sexual.[27]

Though Manuel as he tends his pigs is already restive under an incomprehensible obligation laid upon him by his mother, it is only with the invasion of his life by the spirit of romance, Horvendile, and the power of dreams, Miramon Lluagor, that he repudiates both Suskind and his symbolic position as swineherd. Having thus quietly and unknowingly rebelled against the state of identity with primitive nature, Manuel sets out on the typically Faustian quest for the unattainable princess and ends in a typically Odyssean position—ruler of a kingdom, husband of a shrewd and prudent wife, and father of a noble family.[28]

Not only does the pattern of Manuel's life conform to the general pattern of Cabellian comedy, but he is by every measure the world knows successful. Because, however, Manuel has never truly known his own desire and because no single strand of his life has led to an anticipated consequence, he remains baffled and vaguely dissatisfied. Even so, in typically Odyssean fashion he might have lived out his life in reasonable comfort in the familiar room of Ageus (Usage) if it were not for the fact that from the beginning he has borne a special curse, that of knowing the exact value of whatever he achieved. It is this curse that is fulfilled when Manuel unwittingly opens the magic casement of the window of Ageus.

It is never clear just what Manuel knows or feels, but as he looked through the window of Ageus into the gray, sweetly scented nothingness beyond, he must at least have realized that all he had come to possess was pure illusion, and he may also have guessed that all the restless desire from which he had drawn his immense energies was at bottom only the mistranslated animal-longing for Suskind. At any rate, having looked through the window, Manuel is confronted by a choice; he may return to Suskind, that is, may return to unconscious identity with the elemental forces of life, or he may deliberately embrace the illusions of his human condition. Like Jurgen and Gerald Musgrave, he embraces illusion.[29] Manuel had begun his career by trading upon the Luciferian knowledge that "the world wishes to be deceived"; he ends by affirming this through his own action as profound truth. Manuel's final act, that of killing Suskind in order to protect his family, is a thoroughly Odyssean one, but beyond this, it is in the killing of Suskind, and of Oriander before her, and in the sealing up of the window of Ageus that Manuel actually functions as a redeemer. For by these actions he makes impossible any falling away from the human condition into the condition of primitive unconsciousness and thus, as it were, ensures the perpetual repetition from generation to generation of the comedy of his own life.

In part Suskind may be regarded as the proper mate of the primitive psyche, just as Ettarre is the ideal mate of the human spirit. In killing Suskind, Manuel destroys the dynamics of his own psyche and thereby deprives himself of the energy by which he had lived. Death, however, is welcome to him; after such revelations, life on the old terms is no longer possible.[30] Moreover, death itself is assimilated to the comic point of view by purging it of its aspects of finality and deprivation. In death, as Cabell has noted, man the eternal comedian touches the hem of tragedy's gown. But though Manuel may perish, the life of Manuel does not. It has already passed on into the bodies of Manuel's children in which it will participate in other comedies not essentially different from that in which Manuel himself performed.[31] Moreover, the reader who reads beyond *Figures of Earth* in the Biography knows that Manuel's life was as complete as any man's may be, that duration could bring no essential addition to it, that though his life were extended through all the generations of his descendants, it could be nothing but endlessly redundant.

From this discussion of the structure of the major comedies consideration of *The High Place* and of *The Silver Stallion* has been largely omitted because, despite their respective subtitles—*A Comedy of Disenchantment* and *A Comedy of Redemption*—they are atypical. They are atypical not because they belong to a separate category, but because as compared to *Jurgen, Figures of Earth,* and *Something About Eve* they give us only fragments of what we have come to recognize as the essential pattern of Cabellian comedy. In scope of theme and action they are far more severely circumscribed and far more specialized than the other major comedies. Both are, in a sense, devoted to making explicit specific ideas which underlie or are implicit in the working out of the total comic pattern. Consequently, considered in themselves they are decidedly lesser affairs; considered as parts of the inclusive structure of the Biography, they serve a subordinate function. They provide a perspective upon the other major comedies, focusing for the reader the significance of the action or, at least, parts of the action of these comedies.

Thus, despite its amusing central situation, *The High Place* is in fact little more than an addendum to *Jurgen,* devoted to making explicit the implications of Jurgen's unwonted act of self-abnegation in the presence of the sleeping Helen of his dreams. Florian de Puysange, the protagonist of *The High Place,* plays out the role that Jurgen shrewdly declined; that is, he accepts the seemingly extraordinary favor of fate, arouses not only his sleeping beauty, Melior, but his patron saint, Hoprig, as well, and thus, with predictably disastrous results, brings into his daily life the fleshly embodiments of his ideals of beauty and holiness. In this ill-advised act the Faustian component would seem to have achieved its destructive fulfillment. However, though paradoxically Florian's good fortune drives him deeper and deeper into crime and into a kind of spiritual debauchery—supposedly with him, as with Charteris, a reflex of a frustrated desire for sanctity—his egotistical self-absorption is such that he is capable of registering convincingly only the annoyance and irritability of a discomfited hedonist.

Moreover, Cabell provides in this comedy for a "happy" ending by adopting the ancient dream-vision technique: as it turns out Florian has only dreamed of his fiasco with Melior and Hoprig. The reader is at the end assured that Florian went on to live his life no less dissolutely but somewhat more shrewdly in the shadow of his youthful vision. Clearly, as the story presents only a brief segment of the protagonist's life and that only as lived in anticipation of youthful vision, and as the protagonist himself is a rather flat character, there is no room for the working out of the total characteristic pattern of Cabellian comedy; but the somewhat slight theme of the book—the inevitable failure-in-success attendant upon any supposed fulfillment of the Faustian quest—is in a quite obvious way related to that pattern.

As for *The Silver Stallion*—it is not, strictly speaking, *a* comedy at all. It is a collection of comically presented allegorical tales, each of which is designed to set forth some particular aspect of the world-view which forms the background and the foundation of the Biography. These tales are bound together first by the fact that they all relate experiences which befell various of the followers of Manuel after his death, and secondly, and more importantly, by their somewhat indirect relationship to what emerges in the final section, "At Manuel's Tomb," as the major theme of the book. Simply stated, this theme holds that the human imagination, directed by the imperious need of the human spirit for some vision of a better life and for some promise of salvation, is capable of creating out of the shoddy stuff of reality a beautiful dream of sanctity and redemption. The final irony lies in the fact that in the end all of Manuel's followers, whose motley and maculate experiences have paraded through the book, are willy-nilly absorbed into the legend of Manuel the Redeemer and sanctified by this same ruthless imagination which cares little or nothing for fact or logic or particular personalities. To stress this irony, however, is not to say that *The Silver Stallion* is an inconoclastic satire. Its spirit is genuinely comic, but whereas the other major comedies may be said to celebrate the persistence of the human spirit in an irrational and hostile universe, this one celebrates the persistence of human dreams, celebrates the power of the dream to retain much of its potency and beauty despite denial and hypocrisy, corruption and perversion.

From the Faustian point of view, the flux of the comic protagonist's character and the final allegiance to illusion, which are characteristic of Cabellian comedy, re-enact the old tragic story of the fall from grace once localized in Eden. The reader, however, is made to feel that this fall, inasmuch as it is in the interest of life, is fortunate. For the point of view from which the reader witnesses the action of the comedy is neither Faustian nor Odyssean; rather, it is detached and ironic. Consequently, the reader never approaches more than a partial identity of interest with the comic protagonist in either of his roles. (The fact that the comic protagonist never seems quite to know what he is about and the fantastic terms in which his objectives and desires are expressed ensure this detachment.) Being free from commitment, the reader is also free to enjoy the manifold double meanings and displacements, the radical disjuncture between cause and effect and the disproportion between means and ends which result from the baffling way in which various strands of life compete with one another, flow into one another, and cancel one another out: for the reader the finite predicament—so painful to the Faustian nature —becomes comic in the sense of being laughter-provoking.

More important than this, however, the reader perceives from the beginning that the comic protagonist is playing a game of blindman's buff and that his total interests are not expressed in his Faustian role. He perceives that Freydis and Ettarre have their dark malevolent aspects as surely as does Maya, and that generally behind the appearances with which the comic protagonist has to do, unknowable and probably blind forces are at work.[32] (The very names of the beings encountered by the comic protagonist often convey to the reader a wealth of connotations which is apparently wasted upon the protagonist himself.) At the same time, the reader sees that on the plane of appearances life is capable of blossoming into some rather lovely possibilities which are available to the comic protagonist so long as he doesn't challenge their validity, and also that the demon of the absolute, which is the inseparable companion of the Faustian component, threatens the stability of all appearances. Therefore, from the reader's point of view, though life would be impoverished if the Faustian component had no part in it, its betrayal and loss of power are fortunate so far as the total well-being of the comic protagonist is concerned, and the reader may rejoice in it.

In general what the reader is made to see is that success in the game which the comic protagonist plays consists not in winning through to any substantial goal but in gathering to himself as much as possible of the beauty, the pleasure, and the comfort of appearances without suffering the malice of either Freydis or Maya, without either assuming the cross of disillusionment or sinking to the unconscious animal level. This Jurgen and Gerald Musgrave and, within limits, Manuel succeed in doing. Moreover, the reader is made to see that the very conditions of which the comic protagonist complains—the enigmatic nature of himself and of his world, his irremediable loneliness, and his isolation from reality and truth—are, ironically, the necessary conditions of his success. Thus, the so-called finite predicament not only becomes a source of comic laughter but is itself assimilated as an essential part of the comic pattern. In the Cabellian comic vision the knowledge that "we have heard the key turn in the lock once and once only" ceases to be felt as simply pathetic or tragic and comes to be seen as the grounds for the salvation of the human spirit.

Perennial complaints against the finite predicament echo from generation to generation throughout *The Biography of Manuel*. Insofar as the reader feels with the individual protagonist, the pathos of these complaints is real enough, but nonetheless the reader from his superior angle of vision cannot help perceiving that there is something patently comical in complaining against that which is not only irremediable but beneficent.

When one reads through the Biography as Cabell finally arranged it, he finds the comic vision re-enforced in several ways. The underlying irony of the Biography is that each individual life, for all its felt uniqueness, is merely one more essentially undifferentiated beat in the monotonous rhythm of life flowing down from Manuel. Negatively considered, this is a satire upon all concepts of progress and amelioration, but positively it means that the human spirit endures and with it the dreams and illusions and the comic pattern of life. To be sure, as one follows the life of Manuel from Poictesme to Lichfield the action seems to fall away into the inconsequential; there seems to be a considerable loss of scope and meaning. If, however, the modern Lichfieldians play out their comedies on a much smaller stage, it is not because anything essential has been subtracted from them, but because the free play of the imagination, which is needed to project their comedies upon the plane of symbol and myth, has been circumscribed by realism and scientism. And just as the second book in the Biography, *The Silver Stallion,* gives assurance that human dreams are indomitable and that in their imperiousness and ruthlessness they can thrive upon the most unlikely materials, so the last book, *The Cream of the Jest,* gives assurance that the power of the imagination does not diminish; for those who can avail themselves of it, it can still transfigure human living.

It is difficult to measure out in exact degrees a development such as has been traced here. It is impossible to say when Cabell arrived at the final elaboration of his point of view or by what steps he arrived at his mature style or to what extent, if at all, the elaboration of point of view outran the necessary technical development. It is, however, possible to indicate a pattern of growth and change in the published works.

In the earliest works—*The Line of Love, The Eagle's Shadow,* and *Gallantry*—Cabell's interest seems to have been largely historical and social: his talents seem to have been dominated on the one hand by the comedy of manners and on the other by historical romance. The persistent and dominant subject of these earliest works is the love-marriage sequence, the betrayal of the callow idealism and ardor of youthful love as it declines into the somewhat stodgy domestic comedies of marriage and middle age. This theme, of course, is omnipresent in all of Cabell's works, but at this early stage its implications are not drawn out much beyond the old axiom that love is blind and leads to ironic and comical results.

At least implicit in these earliest works taken as a whole is another theme which suggests that various human experience is at bottom consistently the same. From the beginning, Cabell's imagination was strongly drawn to the personality and fate of the artist and to the culture of two historical periods, the Middle Ages and the eighteenth century, and out of the contemplation of these he apparently developed his concept of the three basic attitudes toward life as well as the conviction that human living, under whatever circumstances, does not vary in essentials. However, because initially Cabell's method was in part that of historical romance, which strives to reproduce the very style and gesture and material circumstance of the period with which it deals, the emphasis in these early works seems to fall upon historical differences rather than upon fundamental similarities.

In the comedies of what we might call the middle period— *The Cords of Vanity, Domnei,* and *The Rivet in Grandfather's Neck* —Cabell continued to work within the given framework of the comedy of manners or of historical romance. However, in these comedies Cabell showed far greater power as an ironist and humorist than in the preceding works. Whereas the humor in the preceding works depended largely upon repartee and wit, in these middle comedies it arises out of the interplay of character and situation; whereas in the preceding works the irony is generally romantic, the reflex of the protagonist's sardonic evaluation of his own condition, in these middle comedies there is an underlying irony which envelops the whole action and eventuates not in pity or mockery but in a greater complexity of view. Moreover, especially in *The Cords of Vanity* and in *The Rivet in Grandfather's Neck,* Cabell displays a surer grasp of complex human psychology, or at any rate is far more successful in rendering human personality subtly and convincingly. The categorical approach to human personality which Cabell had earlier adopted is nominally applied but has already ceased to dominate the portrayal of character. To be sure, Rudolph Musgrave may be classified as chivalrous and Townsend as gallant, but to do so involves modifications and adjustments which serve to make these categories vaguer, less arbitrary.

Considered by themselves, these two books would suggest that Cabell's talent was drifting toward the realistic satire of contemporary manners, but in the perspective provided by the later comedies, it is clear that even in this middle stage Cabell was elaborating the comic pattern and the basic psychology of the comedies written after *The Cream of the Jest.* The psychology of Rudolph Musgrave has strong affinities with that of Manuel and the psychology of Townsend with that of Jurgen, and the story of young Townsend's philanderings dimly foreshadowed the whole essential pattern of *Something About Eve.* What is lacking here is allegorical and mythical dimensions which in the later comedies serve to bring out the universal implications of these particular cases, dissociating them from particular times and mores and making them carry a large burden of metaphysical and psychological meanings.

It is also apparent that by the time Cabell wrote the comedies of the middle period, he had begun to discover the allegorical and symbolic possibilities of fairy-tale and folk-lore materials and techniques. In all three of these comedies he makes tentative and limited use of such techniques and materials for the purpose of focusing the theme and of exposing the hidden springs of the action.

The transitional comedy, *The Cream of the Jest,* is bound to the preceding works by its reliance upon historical materials and upon the historical perspective, but it breaks with them in the use of fantasy: a world of fantasy is held in ironic juxtaposition with the commonplace world of ordinary experience. *The Cream of the Jest,* however, is far from the comic allegorical fantasies which were to follow it. For despite the fantastic structure of Felix Kennaston's private world and the presence in that world of numerous allegorical elements—for instance, the character of Ettarre and her ambiguous relationship to the goddess Isis—the method of the comedy is largely discursive. Moreover, the admitted separation between a private and public world allows the reader to maintain a more or less normal orientation. At the same time, the essential pattern of Cabellian comedy—the awareness of the finite predicament, the struggle to escape the limitations implicit in that predicament, and the final acquiescence in the predicament upon terms of relative contentment—emerges clearly. And here it becomes clear that the naturalistic interpretation of man's situation in the universe is the real background against which Cabellian comedy is played.

In the preceding works naturalistic assumptions and sentiments had often been voiced, but because they were generally assimilated to the mood of the speaker, their exact significance is not clear before this work.

In the comedies which followed *The Cream of the Jest* Cabell broke almost entirely with the techniques of the comedy of manners and of historical romance. In general, whereas in the preceding comedies the themes are reflected upon the plane of recognizable, if not ordinary, human experience, in these late comedies ordinary human experiences are reflected upon the plane of myth and allegory where they become meaningfully related to broad psychological and metaphysical concepts. Structurally these comedies are pure fantasies built out of the boldly adapted materials of folklore and myth. By a complicated blending of the Faust and the Odysseus legends and by the use of ambiguous supernatural beings drawn from and created out of the odds and ends of myth and folklore, Cabell manages to expose the exact conditions, metaphysical and psychological, of the finite predicament as he understands it. Moreover, held in the dual focus of irony, this so-called finite predicament, so rich in incongruities and double meanings, is not only made the source of comic laughter but is itself assimilated as a necessary condition of the comic pattern. Specifically, the reader is placed in a position which enables him to join in that remote laughter to which everything moves, in a position from which he is able to perceive that, ironically, man's susceptibility to illusion, his enigmatic and contradictory nature, and the ambiguity of his situation are precisely the conditions which permit the human spirit to endure in a world largely hostile to it.

8

Cabell in Perspective

In the late nineteenth and early twentieth centuries the influence of philosophical naturalism upon literary theory and practice came to be omnipresent, and both by those who accepted and by those who reacted against it, its voice was heard in general as the newly raised voice of Pan crying folly and delusion to all romantic and humanistic values. The naïve faith of Emile Zola in a scientific novel quickly collapsed before the despair and bitter irony of such a writer as Theodore Dreiser, who with the aid of Herbert Spencer managed to draw some meaning from the concatenation of experience but could not contemplate the resulting vision of life without great pain. Ideals, struggles, deprivations, sorrows, joys?—Dreiser found that these could only be described as "chemic compulsions." Life, human life included?—Dreiser found it a struggle for survival and supremacy or, scientifically apprehended, a momentary equilibrium between the forces of growth and the forces of decay. Once this vision had been granted, Dreiser could only support it and substantiate it, vacillating between a surrender to life through the worship of force and the simple pronouncement that this is not good but it is true.

As Cabell has pointed out in "The Colophon" to *The Way of*

Ecben, to say that all is not well is permitted, is even expected, but thereafter to proffer no panacea is not permitted. By this Cabell meant that, while a Theodore Dreiser may insist upon the whole truth of his chilling and bitter vision, mankind generally must either deny the vision or find some means of transcending it. And, in fact, the history of American literature in the twentieth century would seem, as does all human history, to bear out this assertion; new values have been found, old values revitalized or reinterpreted, all adapted to a changed context of thought and circumstance.

Cabell was one of those who early saw or, perhaps more accurately, felt the need for some transcendent attitude or point of view. He was not inclined to deny, though skepticism held at a distance, the naturalistic vision of life, even as Dreiser had dramatically though ponderously articulated it. Significantly, however, Cabell's earliest subject matter and his earliest source of inspiration were neither the thought nor the circumstances of his contemporary world. They were largely found in the literature of the past and in the admittedly transfigured record which that literature seemed to him to provide of man's thoughts and attitudes. Through this artificial corridor Cabell approached the contemporary, and while the perspective which he thus gained may have been an artificial one, it provided for a largeness and detachment of view denied to such men as Dreiser. For one thing, Cabell saw that the naturalistic vision of life in its essentials is neither startlingly new nor in itself a whole truth; since Ecclesiastes, at least, it has had intermittent currency. And he saw that men had always denied or transcended this vision, that the human spirit had contrived to endure through the substitution of certain dynamic illusions for its discomforting intuitions of reality. He apparently saw too that these illusions received their only really adequate fulfillment in literature, and consequently he came to the conviction that literature is itself in its essential function a means of transcendence.

For Cabell, then, the naturalistic vision needed correction by the addition of the theory of dynamic illusions before it could be said in any sense to express the truth about human living. Philosophical naturalism might split experience into two realms, one of substance and the other of illusion, but it was not thereby justified in conferring reality upon one and denying it to the other. For the history of mankind as well as the histories of individual men are, Cabell came to perceive, records of the human spirit's ambiguous relations with both these realms. To speak the truth about human living one must speak not only of instincts and chemic compulsions but of the goals and ideals which the human spirit has first spun out of itself and then hypostatized, and of the incongruous, disjunctive, and yet in its outcome ironically beneficent interplay of instinct and illusion and time. In other words, he must grasp and somehow express the essential nature of man and the essential pattern of his life.

Cabell's long-standing quarrel with realism and with the advocates of the so-called vital novel stemmed precisely from this conviction. In *Beyond Life* John Charteris is made to admit that the contemporary may legitimately be taken as the subject matter of literature, but only if "through some occult magic, the tale becomes a symbol: and if, however dimly, we comprehend that we are not reading merely about John Jones, aged 26, who gave his address as 187 West Avenue, but about humanity—and about the strivings of that ape reft of his tail, and grown rusty at climbing, who yet, however dimly, feels himself to be a symbol, and the frail representative of Omnipotence in a place that is not home; and so strives blunderingly, from mystery to mystery, with pathetic makeshifts, not understanding anything, greedy in all desires, and honeycombed with poltroonery, and yet ready to give all, and to die fighting, for the sake of that undemonstrable idea. If, in short, the chronicle becomes a symbol of that which is really integral to human existence, in a sense to which motor cars and marriage licenses and even joys and miseries appear as extraneous things— why, then and then only, this tale of our contemporaries shifts incommunicably to fine art. . . ."[1] But this, Cabell contended, is rarely the case. At the time when Cabell was a beginning writer, the apparent drift of realism under the impact of naturalism was toward the chronicling of the minutiae of everyday existence, the slice of life, and toward the exposition and exploration of immediate social and political problems; and from Cabell's point of view this amounted to a betrayal of literature's essential function as providing a means by which man may, at least momentarily, transcend himself and the routine of his existence.

From the same conviction stemmed Cabell's much misunderstood defense of romanticism and of the romantic. At bottom Cabell's romanticism is no more than the instinctive preference of every human being for illusion over truth, and the romantic as literary artist is one who rejects the minutiae of daily routine in favor of those large, irreducibly symbolic figures—Prometheus, Faust, Odysseus—who transcend ordinary human experience but who do, at least partially, express in what they are and in what they do and in what they suffer "that which is really integral to human experience."

Cabell, then, for all that the world-view which forms the necessary background of his comedies has been deeply influenced by naturalistic assumptions, aligned himself with the romantic spirit of man and with the romantic artist as against naturalism because it seemed to him that naturalism exalts a half-truth, and in the name of that half-truth encourages a literary method which is diametrically opposed to the proper function of art. The central one of those dusty truisms which Cabell claims form the foundation of *The Biography of Manuel* is that a man does not live by bread alone but by the dreams and illusions that his imperious and omnivorous need to transcend the implications of his own experience evoke for his salvation; over against the two truths—that we copulate and die—is set a third truth: upon the plane of illusion, the only plane of which man can be immediately aware, this simple physiological basis of life blooms perpetually into something quite different, far more beautiful and more acceptable to the human spirit.

To classify Cabell as a romantic upon the basis of his stated preference can, however, be misleading. Clearly he belongs neither with the major romantics who rejoice in life because they find it good nor with the minor romantics who veil life and present it drenched in transfiguring moonlight because they find it unbearably ugly.[2] He has not retreated from reality to an idealized world; he has retreated to a transcendent world in which the essential pattern of human experience and, as it happens, the comedy of human living can find expression.

A philosopher, Santayana has asserted, who was born a materialist and not plunged into materialism as into a cold bath would be a laughing philosopher. He would be a laughing philosopher because he would have no difficulty in putting life at a distance from him; he would apprehend life as a spectacle, rejoicing in the colorful procession of essences (illusions), accepting without regret what he saw as their transient and insubstantial nature, and laughing over the multiple incongruities, contradictions, and reversals to which the general flux gave rise. For the rest—that life should yield him poetic beauty and practical security—would be enough. By implication, then, both naturalistic despair and its usual antidote, a limited social consciousness, are the by-products of the cold bath. It seems unlikely that Cabell escaped this cold bath altogether, though there is no available record of crises except, perhaps, the gradual transition in his works from a more or less bitter or mocking romantic irony to a complex, impersonal irony. The fact, however, remains that far from succumbing to despair, Cabell declared the essential pattern of human living comic; he "looked into the abyss and laughed," not bitterly but with pleasure, and with pity and tenderness too; and in that laughter he transcended the naturalistic dilemma. Cabell, of course, is not Santayana's hypothetical materialist, but—putting aside the impossible question of temperament—it seems likely that the fact of Cabell's having approached life through history and literature made it possible for him to apprehend life as spectacle, the world as theater, and thus to find in the spectacle an imaginative pleasure relatively unqualified by anxiety.

It is not, however, merely detachment or aloofness which accounts for Cabell's transcendence of the naturalistic dilemma, but wholeness of vision as well. For Theodore Dreiser man is " a mechanism, undevised and uncreated, and a badly and carelessly driven one at that." For Cabell also this may be true, but it is equally and more certainly true that man is a gullible, dreaming consciousness and that the physical processes in which he participates and of which he is an expression are for him perpetually fruitful in moral principles. "So has man's vanity made a harem of his instincts and walled off a seraglio wherein to beget the virtues and refinements and all ennobling factors in man's long progress from gorillaship."[3] Man is cajoled, hoodwinked, and betrayed; yet—behold the miracle!—he is in some sense the better for it. Man wanders blindly through a universe which is largely hostile to him and in which he is subject to the treachery of his own instincts and to the merciless attrition of time; yet—behold the miracle!—the human spirit endures, and endures precisely because of these apparently unamiable conditions.

However, to get at what is really integral to human existence, to get at the essential pattern of human living, obviously involves a high degree of abstraction. For the philosopher it is permissible and necessary to end in abstraction, but for the literary artist it is not permissible. The literary artist must find some means of giving dramatic expression to his vision; he must embody it in specific objects and actions so as to make it available to his reader on something like the level of experience. Cabell solved this problem by turning his back upon verisimilitude, by turning to those vaguely yet complexly symbolic figures out of legend and folklore and myth which have always attracted the romantic, and by adopting a technique of allegorical and symbolic fantasy. The fantasy assures detachment and provides for that frustration of the reader's normal orientation which is necessary if the reader is to transcend both the particularity of human experience and his own prepared responses. The symbolic and allegorical figures with which Cabell worked or from which he modeled his characters bring with them an immediate depth of meaning. They express or suggest segments of the essential pattern without eliciting an immediately personal and possibly irrelevant response. Moreover, because their symbolic value is inexhaustible, they are susceptible to endless rehandling. And, by constantly exploiting the incongruity between their assumed symbolic value and a deliberately inadequate representation of them, Cabell sustains the comic mood; by playing them off one against the other—Odysseus against Faust— he manages to suggest the way in which, in the general flux of character and experience, the tragic implications of existence are cancelled out.

Both this technique and the underlying concept of Cabellian comedy were, however, arrived at only after a long apprenticeship. Only in *Jurgen, Figures of Earth,* and *Something About Eve* is the total essential pattern fully elaborated and articulated with a sureness of touch that comes with the mastery of a personal technique. An examination of these comedies dismisses finally all question as to the propriety of speaking of Cabellian comedy as a distinct variety, one which can be formally defined but which does not fall within the limits of any existing theory. At the same time, it is significant that these three major comedies, though they stand out in *The Biography of Manuel,* do not represent a wholly new departure. They come as the culmination of a line of development that is clearly traceable through the earlier works; consequently, they may justly be taken as at once defining both the goal and the achievement.

In essence, the achievement was the creation of a kind of comedy which threads the line between comedy and tragedy without being tragicomedy. Whereas tragicomedy is a hybrid, depending for its effect upon a last minute reversal by means of which the action is deflected from impending disaster toward an at least unexpectedly happy ending, Cabellian comedy is in its overall effect comic, despite frequent modulations in tone and mood. Like all seriously intended comedy, Cabellian comedy may be said to rejoice over the endless fertility of life, but unlike most comedy, it expresses a comic vision which has been arrived at not by exclusion but by inclusion. It approaches tragedy in its attempt to transcend the whole of the finite predicament (for Cabell, the naturalistic dilemma) and thereby to reconcile man to his role in the scheme of things.

Notes

Chapter 1

1. P. 221 (see List of Works Cited for full bibliographical information).
2. Pp. 496-502.
3. Hooker, "Something About Cabell," p. 200.
4. Cargill, p. 502.
5. Hoffman, *The Modern Novel in America,* p. 119.
6. Pp. 339-52.
7. Pp. 251-61.
8. April 21, 1956.
9. "James Branch Cabell," p. 330.
10. *The American Novel and Its Tradition,* pp. viii-ix.
11. "James Branch Cabell," pp. 200-206.
12. P. 345.
13. "On Not Having Read James Branch Cabell," pp. 597-99.

Chapter 2

1. "Mr. Cabell's Cosmos," pp. 278-79.
2. *Beyond Life,* pp. 38-39.
3. *The Cream of the Jest,* p. 139.
4. Pp. 84-85.
5. P. 127.
6. *The Modern Temper,* p. 21.
7. Vaihinger, *The Philosophy of "As If,"* pp. 44, 84, 330.
8. Cabell, *Smire,* p. 295.
9. Schlipp, *Philosophy of George Santayana,* p. 497.
10. *Beyond Life, passim.*
11. Vaihinger, p. 12.
12. Santayana, *Soliloquies in England and Later Soliloquies,* p. 123.
13. Vaihinger, p. 380.
14. *Beyond Life,* pp. 33, 201.
15. *Smire,* p. 294.
16. *Beyond Life;* Santayana, *Interpretation of Poetry and Religion.*
17. *Beyond Life,* pp. 30-31; *Jurgen,* pp. 132-36; *Something About Eve, passim.*
18. Santayana, *The Life of Reason,* II, 30.
19. Santayana, *Scepticism and Animal Faith,* p. 64; *Beyond Life,* pp. 316 ff.

20. Schlipp, p. 364.
21. *Beyond Life,* pp. 36, 67-95, 101.
22. For Santayana's classification of "dispositions" see "Apologia Pro Mente Sua," in Schlipp, pp. 497-605.
23. *Ibid.,* p. 557; cf. Cabell, *Preface to the Past,* pp. 33 ff.
24. Schlipp, p. 548.
25. Santayana, *Life of Reason,* II, 30; cf. Cabell, *These Restless Heads,* p. 194.
26. *Winds of Doctrine,* p. 49.
27. Pp. 44, 300.
28. Munitz, *The Moral Philosophy of Santayana,* p. vi.
29. *These Restless Heads,* p. 163.
30. Santayana, *Platonism and the Spiritual Life,* p. 40; Cabell, *Straws and Prayer-books,* pp. 26-27, 175-202.
31. *Beyond Life,* p. 267.

Chapter 3

1. *Basic Writings of Sigmund Freud,* pp. 797-98.
2. *Essays and Soliloquies,* pp. 108-12, 191.
3. Barea, *Unamuno,* p. 35.
4. *Soliloquies in England,* p. 142.
5. *Preface to the Past,* p. 34.
6. *Smire,* p. 105.
7. *Special Delivery,* p. 268.
8. *Beyond Life,* p. 18.
9. *Essays and Soliloquies,* pp. 85, 156.
10. *These Restless Heads,* p. 163.
11. *Scepticism and Animal Faith,* p. 75.
12. *Platonism and the Spiritual Life,* p. 30.
13. *Soliloquies in England,* p. 141.
14. *Ibid.,* p. 66.
15. P. 171.
16. "The Biography of Manuel," p. 1109.

Chapter 4

1. *Laughter,* pp. 5, 87, 136.
2. Pp. 45, 46.
3. P. 15.
4. *The Comic Spirit in Meredith,* pp. 4-5.

5. Pp. 114-91 *passim.*

6. *An Aristotelian Theory of Comedy,* pp. 80, 181, 182, 200.

7. *The Nature of Comedy,* pp. 8, 38, 81, 131, 169.

8. *The Dark Voyage and the Golden Mean,* pp. 39, 45, 174-75.

9. *In Praise of Comedy,* pp. 112-16.

10. *Beyond Life,* p. 18.

11. *Preface to the Past,* p. 36.

12. *Straws and Prayer-books,* pp. 73-109.

13. *These Restless Heads,* p. 160.

14. *The Great Tradition,* p. 221.

15. "A Key to Cabell," p. 437.

16. "James Branch Cabell, Romancier," pp. 230-31.

17. *Panaroma de la littérature américaine contemporaine,* pp. 179-80.

18. Pp. 3-18.

19. P. 48.

20. P. xx (italics added).

21. *Beyond Life,* pp. 263-64; *Soliloquies in England,* p. 2.

22. Schlipp, p. 102.

23. Cabell, *The Certain Hour,* p. 1.

24. Feibleman, p. 92.

25. *Ibid.,* p. 183.

26. *The Nature of Comedy,* pp. 170-72.

27. *Preface to the Past,* p. 33.

28. Santayana, *Soliloquies in England,* p. 141.

29. *Preface to the Past,* p. 32.

30. *Ibid.,* pp. 32-34.

31. *In Praise of Comedy,* pp. 119, 205.

32. P. 202.

33. *Preface to the Past,* pp. 33-34.

34. *In Praise of Comedy,* pp. 205-6.

35. *The Dark Voyage,* p. 175.

36. *Ibid.,* p. 35.

37. *The Certain Hour,* pp. 9-10.

38. Cabell, *The Silver Stallion,* pp. 53-81.

39. *These Restless Heads,* pp. 3-21, 233-49.

Chapter 5

1. *Preface to the Past,* pp. 244-45.

2. *Ibid.,* p. 27.

3. *Ibid.,* p. 105.

4. *Straws and Prayer-books,* p. 270.

5. Pp. 26, 263 (1905 ed.); pp. 52, 228 (Storisende ed.).

6. P. 266 (Storisende ed.).

7. Pp. 116, 156.

8. Kalki ed., pp. 89-111.

9. *Preface to the Past,* pp. 201-2.

10. Pp. 193-94, 225.

11. Pp. 122-28.

12. *Preface to the Past,* p. 134.

13. Pp. 61-87.

14. P. 181.

15. See pp. 137-67, 245-72.

16. *Preface to the Past,* pp. 202-3.

17. *Gallantry,* p. xxvi.

18. *Preface to the Past,* pp. 125-26.

19. *The Cream of the Jest,* p. 13.

Chapter 6

1. *Beyond Life,* pp. 250-51.

2. P. 110.

3. Pp. 116-30.

4. P. 348.

5. P. 127.

6. Pp. 258-59.

7. P. 207.

8. P. 3.

9. Pp. 6-11.

10. Pp. 34-37.

11. Pp. 79, 293.

12. *Preface to the Past,* pp. 285-86.

13. Pp. 196-97.

14. Baring-Gould, *Curious Myths of the Middle Ages,* pp. 240 ff.

15. *Ibid.,* p. 12.

16. "Mr. Cabell's Farewell," pp. 201-2.

17. See *The Eagle's Shadow,* p. 173; *Gallantry,* p. 181; *The Cords of Vanity,* p. 307.

18. *Psyche and Symbol,* pp. 61 ff.

19. *Preface to the Past,* pp. 126-27, 205.

20. *Ibid.,* p. 117.

21. *The Certain Hour,* pp. 113-35.

22. P. 13.

23. P. 116.

24. Pp. 137, 139.

25. Pp. 86, 107-10, 116-17.

26. Pp. 151-52, 153-58.

27. P. 190.

28. P. 216.   29. P. 206.

30. Pp. 159-62, 215-17.

31. P. 235.

Chapter 7

1. *Preface to the Past,* pp. 65-68.
2. *Psyche and Symbol,* pp. 58-60.
3. *Something About Eve,* pp. 166, 276.
4. P. 139.
5. *Something About Eve,* pp. 232-33.
6. *Jurgen,* pp. 291-96.
7. *Something About Eve,* p. 97.
8. *Figures of Earth,* pp. 252-59.
9. *Something About Eve,* pp. 278-79.
10. Also *The Silver Stallion,* pp. 147-76.
11. *Something About Eve,* pp. 281-83.
12. *Straws and Prayer-books,* pp. 113-25; *The Way of Ecben.*
13. *Something About Eve,* pp. 113-19.
14. *Jurgen,* pp. 172-73, 206-7, 316-29.
15. *Ibid.,* p. 318.
16. *Ibid.,* pp. 125-27.
17. *Ibid.,* pp. 223-25, 296.
18. *Something About Eve,* pp. 57-62; cf. pp. 282-83.
19. *Psyche and Symbol,* pp. 135-36.
20. *Something About Eve,* p. 266.
21. *Jurgen,* pp. 320-21.
22. *Something About Eve,* p. 76.
23. *The Cream of the Jest,* p. 223.
24. *Jurgen,* pp. 361-63.
25. *The Silver Stallion,* pp. 308-12; *Something About Eve,* pp. 86-87.
26. *Preface to the Past,* p. 29.
27. *Figures of Earth,* pp. 17, 275-78.
28. *Ibid.,* pp. 4-9.
29. *Ibid.,* pp. 279-86.
30. *Ibid.,* pp. 286-88.
31. *Ibid.,* p. 4; cf. pp. 292-93.
32. See *The High Place,* pp. 155-65; *The Way of Ecben,* pp. 141-43.

Chapter 8

1. P. 201.
2. Cabell, *Some of Us,* pp. 20-24.
3. *Beyond Life,* p. 35.

List of Works Cited

Allen, Gay Wilson. "Jurgen and Faust," *Sewanee Review,* XXXIX (Oct.-Dec., 1931), 485-92.

Barea, Arturo, *Unamuno.* New Haven: Yale University Press, 1952.

Baring-Gould, Sabine. *Curious Myths of the Middle Ages.* New York: John B. Alden, 1885.

Beach, Joseph Warren. *The Comic Spirit in Meredith.* New York, 1911.

Bellamy, John Edward. "James Branch Cabell: A Critical Consideration of His Reputation." Ph.D. dissertation, University of Illinois, 1954.

Bergson, Henri. *Laughter: An Essay on the Meaning of the Comic,* trans. Claudseley Brereton. New York: Macmillan Co., 1912.

Bierstadt, Edward H. "James Branch Cabell," *Bookman,* LVI (Feb., 1923), 741-45.

Brewster, Paul G. "*Jurgen* and *Figures of Earth* and the Russion Shazki," *American Literature,* XIII, 305-18.

Cabell, [James] Branch. *The First American Gentleman.* London: John Lane, 1943.

————. *Ladies and Gentlemen: A Parcel of Reconsiderations.* New York: Robert M. McBride and Co., 1937.

————. *Smire: An Acceptance in the Third Person.* New York: Doubleday, Doran and Co., 1937.

————. *Smirt: An Urbane Nightmare.* New York: Robert M. McBride and Co., 1934.

Cabell, [James] Branch. *Some of Us: An Essay in Epitaphs.* New York: Robert M. McBride and Co., 1930.

————. *Special Delivery: A Packet of Replies.* New York: Robert M. McBride and Co., 1933.

————. *These Restless Heads: A Trilogy of Romantics.* New York: The Literary Guild, 1932.

Cabell, James Branch. *The Certain Hour.* New York: Robert M. McBride and Co., 1923.

————. "The Last Cry of Romance," *Nation,* CXX (May 6, 1925), 521-22.

————. *The Line of Love.* New York: Harper and Brothers, 1905.

————. *Preface to the Past.* New York: Robert M. McBride and Co., 1936.

————. *Quiet, Please.* Gainesville: University of Florida Press, 1952.

————. *The Way of Ecben.* New York: Robert M. McBride and Co., 1929.

————. *Works* (Storisende Edition), 18 vols. New York: Robert M. McBride and Co., 1927-30.

———— and Ellen Glasgow. *An Inscribed Portrait.* New York: Maverick Press, 1938.

Cargill, Oscar. *Intellectual America.* New York: Macmillan Co., 1941.

Chase, Richard. *The American Novel and Its Tradition.* New York: Doubleday Anchor Books, 1957.

Cook, Albert. *The Dark Voyage and the Golden Mean.* Cambridge: Harvard University Press, 1949.

Cooper, Lane. *An Aristotelian Theory of Comedy.* New York: Harcourt, Brace and Co., 1922.

Cover, James P. *Notes on Jurgen.* New York: Robert M. McBride and Co., 1927.

———— and George Cranwell. *Notes on Figures of Earth.* New York: Robert M. McBride and Co., 1929.

Feibleman, James. *In Praise of Comedy: A Study in Its Theory* and *Practice.* London: George Allen and Unwin, 1939.

Freud, Sigmund. *The Basic Writings,* trans. and ed. Dr. A. A. Brill. New York: The Modern Library, 1938.

Glasgow, Ellen. "The Biography of Manuel," *Saturday Review of Literature,* VI (1930), 1108-9.

Gunther, John J. "James Branch Cabell: An Introduction," *Bookman,* XLII (Nov., 1920), 200-206.

Hatcher, Harlan. "On Not Having Read James Branch Cabell," *Bookman,* Feb., 1931, pp. 597-99.

Hergesheimer, Joseph. "James Branch Cabell," *American Mercury,* XIII (Jan., 1928), 38-47.

Hicks, Granville. *The Great Tradition.* New York: Macmillan Co., 1933.

Hoffman, Frederick J. *The Modern Novel in America, 1900-1950.* Chicago: Henry Regnery Co., 1951.

Homer. *Odyssey,* trans. E. V. Rieu. Harmondsworth: Penguin Books, 1946.

Hooker, Edward N. "Something About Cabell," *Sewanee Review,* XXXVII (Apr.-June, 1929), 193-203.

Jung, Carl G. *Psyche and Symbol: A Selection from the Writings,* ed. Violet S. de Laszlo. New York: Doubleday Anchor Books, 1958.

Krutch, Joseph Wood. *The Modern Temper.* New York: Harcourt, Brace and Co., 1929.

Le Breton, Maurice. "James Branch Cabell, Romancier," *Revue Anglo-Américaine,* Oct., 1933, Feb., 1934, pp. 112-28, 223-37.

Lovett, Robert M. "Mr. James Branch Cabell," *New Republic,* XXVI (Apr. 13, 1921), 187-89.

Lueders, Edward. *Carl Van Vechten and the Twenties.* Albuquerque: University of New Mexico Press, 1955.

McIntyre, C. F. "Mr. Cabell's Cosmos," *Sewanee Review,* XXXVIII (July-Sept., 1930), 278-85.

McNeill, Warren A. *Cabellian Harmonics.* New York: Random House, 1928.

Mencken, H. L. *James Branch Cabell.* New York: Robert M. McBride and Co., 1927.

Meredith, George. "On the Idea of Comedy and of the Uses of the Comic Spirit," *Works.* New York: Charles Scribner's Sons, 1910.

Michaud, Régis. *Panorama de la littérature américaine contemporaine.* Paris: Editions Kra, 1926.

Munitz, Milton K. *The Moral Philosophy of Santayana.* New York: Columbia University Press, 1939.

Parker, William R. "A Key to Cabell," *English Journal,* XXI (June, 1932), 431-40.

Parks, Edd. "James Branch Cabell," *Southern Renascence,* ed. L. D. Rubin and R. D. Jacobs. Baltimore: John Hopkins Press, 1953.

——. *Segments of Southern Thought.* Athens: University of Georgia Press, 1938.

Parrington, Vernon L. "The Incomparable Mr. Cabell," *Main Currents in American Thought,* III, 335-45.

Rothman, Julius L. "A Glossorial Index to the *Biography of Manuel.*" Ph.D. dissertation, Columbia University, 1954.

Santayana, George. *Interpretation of Poetry and Religion.* New York: Charles Scribner's Sons, 1905.

——. *The Life of Reason, 2 vols.* New York: Charles Scribner's Sons, 1905.

——. *Platonism and the Spiritual Life.* New York: Charles Scribner's Sons, 1927.

——. *Scepticism and Animal Faith.* New York: Charles Scribner's Sons, 1923.

——. *Soliloquies in England and Later Soliloquies.* New York: Charles Scribner's Sons, 1922.

——. *The Winds of Doctrine.* New York: Charles Scribner's Sons, 1913.

Schlipp, Paul A. (ed.) *The Philosophy of George Santayana.* New York: Charles Scribner's Sons, 1951.

Smith, Willard. *The Nature of Comedy.* Boston: The Gorham Press, 1930.

Tate, Allen. "Mr. Cabell's Farewell," *New Republic,* LXI, (Jan. 8, 1930), 201-2.

Unamuno, Miguel de. *Essays and Soliloquies,* trans. J. E. Crawford Fitch. New York: Alfred A. Knopf, 1925.

Vaihinger, Hans. *The Philosophy of "As If,"* trans. C. K. Ogden. New York: Harcourt, Brace and Co., 1924.

Van Doren, Carl. *James Branch Cabell.* New York: Robert M. McBride and Co., 1932.

Wagenknecht, Edward. *The Calvacade of the American Novel.* New York: Henry Holt and Co., 1952.

Walpole, Hugh. "The Art of James Branch Cabell," *Yale Review,* IX (1919-20), 684-98.

Wilson, Edmund. "The James Branch Cabell Case Reopened," *New Yorker,* XXXII (Apr. 21, 1956), 129-56.

Index

36, 37; divine, 37, 38, 53, 54; serene, 37-38, 55, 56, 57; of disillusionment, 44-45, 47; romantic, 49, 50; sentimental, 64-65

—Cabellian: structure of, 8, 25, 55, 56, 97, 103, 120, 128; subject matter of, 30, 39, 42, 48, 60-61, 64; defined, 31; function of, 39, 40, 45, 46-48, 49, 51-52, 61, 136; protagonist in, 42, 58, 59, 86, 109-18 *passim*, 123-25; point of view of, 47, 49, 54-55, 58, 61-62, 94, 103, 104, 124, 125; basic situation in, 48, 86, 106-7; theory of, compared, 38, 50-51, 53-55, 57, 59, 136; success in, 59-60; basic theme of, 85; techniques of, 103, 104, 119; mentioned, 6, 41, 108

"Concerning Corinna," 95

Cook, Albert: his theory of comedy, 30, 31, 36-37, 52, 55, 56, 59, 110

Cooper, Lane: his theory of comedy, 35, 51

Cords of Vanity, The, 77, 78-82, 83, 84, 85-87, 92, 94, 111, 127

Cosmic chill, 93

Cream of the Jest, The: a transitional comedy, 94-104; mentioned, 12, 67, 77, 91, 92, 126, 128, 129

DEMIURGE, 14, 17

Disillusionment: the nature of, 44-45; mentioned, 20, 62, 75, 89, 112, 116, 125

Divine Comedy, the, 37, 53-54

Domnei, 50, 77, 88-89, 90-91, 94, 95

Dreiser, Theodore, 11, 12, 130, 131, 135

Eagle's Shadow, The, 64, 72, 73-74, 75, 78, 126

Ecclesiastes, 24, 131

"Epilogue of True Thomas by Moonlight," 60

Ettarre: role of, 97, 109, 112, 121, 128; symbolism of, 98, 99, 100, 101; malevolence of, 124

FAIRY TALE: Cabell's use of, 83, 94, 106, 107. *See also* Folklore

Fantasy: comic, 65

Faust, 66, 109, 133

Feibleman, James: his theory of

comedy, 31, 33-34, 37, 40, 48, 49-50, 53, 54

Fictions: defined, 14, 15. *See also* Illusions

Figures of Earth, 50, 108, 109-18 *passim,* 121, 122, 136

First Gentleman of America, The, 43

Folklore: Cabell's use of, 65, 66, 78, 90, 104, 106, 135; interpretation of (Jung), 94, 101, 107, 108; mentioned, 84, 103, 129

Freud, Sigmund, 24, 40

Freydis: symbolism of, 115; malevolence of, 124; mentioned, 85, 108, 125

GALLANT attitude (gallantry): defined, 17-18, 77; predominance of, 68, 75-76; psychology of, 75, 78

Gallantry, 68, 72, 73, 74-76, 78, 89

Gerald Musgrave (character): as comic protagonist, 17, 41, 42, 44, 45, 60, 109-18 *passim*

Glasgow, Ellen, 28

Graustark romance, 69

Gunther, John J.: quoted, 6-7

HAMLET, 30

Hatcher, Harlan: quoted, 7

Hedonism, 21, 80

Helen (of Troy): Cabell's use of, 79, 108, 109, 112, 114, 122

Henry Esmond (Thackeray), 73

Hicks, Granville, 3, 41, 42

High Place, The, 50, 105, 122-23

Horvendile: origin of, 73-74, 76; function of, 91; symbolism of, 101; mentioned, 54, 102, 108, 119, 120

ILLUSIONS: source of, 14, 15, 23, 112, 113; dynamic, 14, 41, 131; instability of, 16; value of, 19, 103, 111, 118, 133; in Cabell's novels, 57, 86, 87, 88, 91, 92, 97, 115, 119, 134; Faustian, 112, 114; Odyssean, 116

"In Necessity's Mortar," 71, 72

"In Ursula's Garden," 72

Irony: defined, 42, 43-44; in Cabell's novels, 61, 69, 72, 74, 78-85 *passim*, 88, 89, 93, 96, 102, 123, 125, 127, 129, 134; tragic, 62; comic, 64, 67; romantic, 71, 111

Isis (Egyptian goddess), 101

Smith, Willard: his theory of comedy, 36, 42, 50, 51
Solipsism, 99
Some of Us, 12
Something About Eve, 83, 105, 108, 113, 114, 115, 122, 128, 136
Soul of Melicent, The, 77
Spencer, Herbert, 130
Spirit: viewpoint of, 14, 26-27, 45; comic, 32, 33
Suskind: symbolism of, 120, 121
Swift, Jonathan, 43

TANNHAUSER, 115
Tate, Allen, 92, 93
Tempest, The: as serene comedy, 37, 56-58; mentioned, 72
"Townsend of Lichfield," 87
Tragedy, 51-52, 56, 61-62, 107, 136
Tragicomedy, 136

Tyl Ulenspiegel, 39

UNAMUNO, Miguel de: tragic vision of, 24-25; mentioned, 13

VAIHINGER, Hans: and Cabell compared, 13, 14, 20, 21
Van Dorn, Carl, 2, 73
Villon, François, 68, 72

WANDERING JEW, 66, 91. *See also* Ahasueras
Way of Ecben, The, style of, 68, 105
"Wedding Jest, The," 50, 68, 70
White Robe, The, style of, 68, 105
Wilde, Oscar, 74
Witch-woman: nature of, 90

ZOLA, Emile, 130